AN
UNCOMMON
FAITH

GEORGE H. SHRIVER

LECTURE SERIES IN

RELIGION IN

AMERICAN HISTORY

NO. 8

AN UNCOMMON FAITH

A PRAGMATIC APPROACH
TO THE STUDY OF
AFRICAN AMERICAN
RELIGION

Eddie S. Glaude Jr.

THE UNIVERSITY OF
GEORGIA PRESS
Athens

Chapter 1 appears in slightly different form in Eddie S. Glaude Jr.,
African American Religion: A Very Short Introduction (New York: Oxford
University Press, 2014). © Oxford University Press 2014. Reprinted
by permission of Oxford University Press, www.oup.com. Chapter 2
appears in slightly different form in Eddie S. Glaude Jr., "Babel
in the North: Black Migration, Moral Community, and the Ethics
of Racial Authenticity," in *A Companion to African American Studies*,
edited by Lewis R. Gordon and Jane Anna Gordon (Hoboken, N.J.:
Blackwell Publishing, 2006). © 2006 by Blackwell Publishing Ltd.

© 2018 by the University of Georgia Press
Athens, Georgia 30602
www.ugapress.org
All rights reserved
Set in 10/14 Quadraat OT Regular by
Kaelin Chappell Broaddus

Most University of Georgia Press titles are
available from popular e-book vendors.

Printed digitally

Library of Congress Cataloging-in-Publication Data

Names: Glaude, Eddie S., Jr., 1968– author.
Title: An uncommon faith : a pragmatic approach to the study of
African American religion / Eddie S. Glaude, Jr.
Description: Athens, Georgia : University of Georgia Press, [2018] |
Series: George H. Shriver lecture series in religion in American
history ; no. 8 | Includes bibliographical references and index.
Identifiers: LCCN 2018004213| ISBN 9780820354897 (hardcover: alk.
paper) | ISBN 9780820354170 (paperback : alk. paper) |
ISBN 9780820354163 (ebook)
Subjects: LCSH: African Americans—Religion—Study and teaching. |
Methodology. | Pragmatism.
Classification: LCC BR563.N4 G595 2018 | DDC 200.89/96073—dc23
LC record available at https://lccn.loc.gov/2018004213

FOR MY MOM AND DAD,

Juanita Glaude and Eddie S. Glaude Sr.

AND OUR AMAZING LITTLE TOWN,

Moss Point, Mississippi

CONTENTS

FOREWORD

The chapters in this book formed the basis for the 2016 George H. Shriver Lectures: Religion in American History delivered at Stetson University on March 29–30. This lecture series, which began in 2000, was endowed through the generosity of Dr. George H. Shriver, Professor of History Emeritus at Georgia Southern University, and an alumnus of Stetson University. The endowment fund established by George Shriver also provided for the publication of each of the lectures. The 2016 lectures, titled "The Study of African American Religion," were the ninth set in this series and were presented by Dr. Eddie S. Glaude Jr., chair of the Department for African American Studies and the William S. Tod Professor of Religion and African American Studies at Princeton University.

The purpose of the Shriver Lectures is to focus on the various ways that religion has shaped and contributed to American culture and history. In keeping with that aim, past speakers in the Shriver Lectures have focused on American Protestantism, the creation-evolution debate, American Judaism, the American encounter with Islam, religion and the American presidents, sports and religion, and the scholarly study of religion in America. In the three lectures delivered in March 2016, the nucleus of the chapters in the present volume, Professor Eddie Glaude Jr. explored another significant dimension of the American religious landscape: the character and complexity of the religious experiences of African Americans. In the first chapter of the book, Glaude describes what he calls a "pragmatic approach to the study of African American religion," characterized by three key ideas: a distinctive practice of freedom in which black religious imagination opens up "spaces closed down by white supremacy"; a sign of difference in which African American religion rejects "the idolatry of white supremacy by proclaiming itself, in practice, as different"; and open-endedness, in which it "offers resources for African Americans to imagine themselves beyond the constraints of now." The second chapter illustrates Glaude's way of telling the story of African American religious history. He challenges a popular understanding of the changes in the African American community, and specifically the changing role of African American churches, as a result of the Black Migration to the North in the 1920s and 1930s. Finally, in the third chapter, Glaude presents W. E. B. Du Bois as a prime example of one that possessed what he calls an "uncommon faith" that has been present in the African American community, a belief "in the capacities of broken people, those who have been profoundly wounded by the reality of white supremacy in this country, to seek better and more excellent versions of who they take themselves to be."

I wish to express my gratitude to Professor Glaude not only for the outstanding lectures he presented but also for his warm and generous spirit. Having him on our campus to enlighten, challenge, and engage us was truly a pleasure. On behalf of Stetson University, I want to express again sincere appreciation to George Shriver for his unselfish gifts that established this lecture series. The presence of George and his wife, Cathy, at the lectures was as an added pleasure. Words of thanks are also due to Dr. Wendy Libby, president of Stetson University, for her support of the lectures and her hosting of a dinner at her home for Dr. Glaude; to Dr. Paul Croce, professor of history at Stetson University, for his assistance as a member of the Shriver Lecture Committee; to Lisa Guenther, administrative specialist in the Department of Religious Studies, for her usual adroit handling of the logistical details for the lectures; and to the University of Georgia Press, and especially to Bethany Snead, for the publication of these lectures.

Mitchell G. Reddish, Chair
George H. Shriver Lectures Committee
Stetson University

ACKNOWLEDGMENTS

My heartfelt thanks to the Stetson University History Department and Department of Religious Studies for the invitation to deliver the Shriver Lectures in March 2016. I am particularly indebted to Mitchell Reddish. His generosity of spirit and general hospitality made my visit all the more special. I was especially delighted by the presence of George and Cathy Shriver. They were wonderfully engaged over the course of my three lectures. I also want to thank Devin Allen for allowing me to use his powerful image for the cover of this book and my colleague Keeanga-Yamahtta Taylor for introducing me to his genius. I am just thrilled that *An Uncommon Faith* includes the extraordinary work of El Anatsui. I have been struggling with the brilliance of Anatsui since my first encounter with his work. I am forever indebted to my colleague Chika Okeke-Agulu for introducing me to his genius and helping me gain permission to include his artwork in the book.

I also want to thank Kevin Wolfe for taking the time to read and comment on the lectures. And thanks to Brown University for inviting me to deliver the K. Brooke Anderson lecture in 2013. This occasioned my first public attempt to think carefully about Du Bois and his haunting essay "Of the Passing of the First-Born." Finally, special thanks to the patient editors at the University of Georgia Press, Bethany Snead and Jon Davies; my amazing copy editor, Sarah C. Smith; and Ana M. Jimenez-Moreno, a Mellon Diversity Fellow who dealt graciously with my bureaucratic ineptitude.

AN
UNCOMMON
FAITH

Pragmatic Beginnings

My serious engagement with pragmatism began in a readings course on the subject with Cornel West at Princeton University. A few of us gathered in a small seminar room in Dickinson Hall where the Program in African American Studies was nestled in a corner next to the Program in Women Studies, desperately trying to keep the History Department from annexing its meager offices. Back then Dickinson had the feeling of an old academic building. Nothing fancy. Just us, scratched-up tables, uncomfortable chairs, and the books. We worked our way through the classical pragmatists up to Richard Rorty and a few others. West was in the last stages of completing his important book *The American Evasion of Philosophy: A Genealogy of Pragmatism*, in which he traced the philosophical tradition from Ralph Waldo Emerson to his own prophetic version of pragmatism. The book was our syllabus and my introduction to pragmatism.

American pragmatism is a philosophical approach that guides how I see the world and how I interpret the problems people, especially black people, face. In this sense, pragmatism, rightly understood, is a form of cultural criticism "in which the meaning of America is put forward by intellectuals in response to distinct social and cultural crises."[1] Here West echoes John Dewey. Dewey believed adamantly that philosophy should be considered a method of identifying and interpreting the serious problems that interrupt our living and that it should offer up ways for dealing with those problems. He believed philosophy ought to be seen as "a method of moral and political diagnosis and prognosis."[2] He is absolutely right.

But Dewey has his blind spots. Three criticisms come immediately to mind. First, Dewey reads as if he overestimates the capacity of human beings to transform their worlds. The exercise of critical intelligence, as Kenneth Burke once suggested, is seemingly his answer to everything. This view smacks of an easy optimism that ignores the darker dimensions of human experience. Second, one wonders what exactly is Dewey's social theory, his understanding of power, and the material conditions that frustrate our efforts to secure certain goods. People do nasty things in pursuit of selfish ends. And black people know this intimately. But Dewey says little about power and is relatively silent about race (even though he was among the founding members of the NAACP). He gives scant attention to the workings of white supremacy in the United States. In doing so, and this is the third criticism, he fails to take seriously the consequences of this insidious ideology for any vibrant and effective theory of democracy. What might it suggest that the preeminent philosopher of American democracy is relatively silent about the central contradictions that undermine his view?

I have sought to find resources within the pragmatist tradition to address these concerns and to answer this question. What has emerged over the years is a particular reading of the tradition and of Dewey, with an emphasis on (1) a morally motivated experimentalism (we tinker in light of problems faced in explicit pursuit of a more just world), (2) a chastened voluntarism (an unyielding faith in our capacities to be otherwise as we acknowledge how broken we actually are), and (3) a radical historicism (we approach history and its meanings, without appeal to "philosophic" foundations, in order to discover how that history might serve or constrain us in our pursuit of a more just world). Each informs the way I approach the study of African American religion. Each is on full display in these George Shriver lectures.

The first chapter, "Pragmatism and African American Religion," lays bare my approach. I want the reader to see the phrase "African American religion" as a tool of the scholar whose aim is to interpret how religious languages in African American communities have been used to respond to white supremacy in this country. The chapter also reflects my effort to deploy (to tinker with) John Dewey's distinction between "religion" and "the religious" in A Common Faith in order to bring into view what I am calling "a black religious attitude," that is, a fundamental shift in the center of gravity in one's self-understanding that has political implications for a world organized on the assumption that white people matter more than others.

The second chapter, "Babel in the North: Black Migration, Moral Community, and the Ethics of Racial Authenticity," seeks to demonstrate that particular histories of African American religion often narrow what we take to be the substance of African American religion (because those histories primarily focus on Afro-Protestantism). I examine a standard story of the role and function of black churches during the interwar period, and I try to show what gets obscured because of standing assumptions about what African American religion is or what it ought to be. The aim is to open up space for consideration of *an ethic of racial authenticity*, a particular instantiation of a black religious attitude. In this chapter, the reader will also see how I approach the writing of African American religious history.

The last chapter, "An Uncommon Faith: Rereading W. E. B. Du Bois on Religion," finally makes clear what motivates the lectures. Throughout the first two chapters Du Bois looms in the shadows. Here I engage him explicitly through a brief but close reading of his essay "Of the Passing of the First-Born," in *The Souls of Black Folk*. I argue that Du Bois represents a third way between Dewey's view of the religious and William James's insistence that religion is, at its root, a cry for help. Confronting his son in the coffin and facing unimaginable grief, Du Bois puts forward a new religious ideal grounded in a recognition of profound brokenness. That religious ideal reorients black people to a world that seeks to consign them to the bottom rungs. It is a religious attitude colored a deep shade of blue.

||||||||||||||||||

I learned so much in that small seminar room in Dickinson Hall. From Anna Julia Cooper and W. E. B. Du Bois to Cornel West, African Americans have engaged pragmatism in the full light of the history and political economy of white supremacy in the United States. Ours have not been a singular concern with the traditional questions of professional philosophy. Instead, we have taken up pragmatism in order to address the complex challenges of the value gap (the belief that white people matter more than others) to the very idea of democracy. In our hands, pragmatism encounters the underside of American life; it assumes the tragic dimensions of our living; it begins with the complex interplay of individual assertion and structural limitations; and it takes for granted the necessity for a fuller grasp of white supremacy and other forms of domination that shape our self-understanding and constitute the backdrop to efforts at self-creation.

Devin Allen's photograph on the cover of this book captures that focus. A young black man stands defiantly as he protests the murder of Freddie Gray in Baltimore. Upside down and draped around his shoulders is the United States flag and written in the white stripes (the gaps) are the names of our dead. His stance draws my attention. His arms are up as if, like the young people in Ferguson, he is shouting the words, "Hands up, don't shoot." But they also look like he is preparing to fly, like Milkman in Song of Solomon, to soar in spite of the evil he directly confronts. This is the stance, the attitude—the disposition—that motivates this book; it is an uncommon faith.

Pragmatism and
African American Religion

American pragmatists have often found themselves grappling with the subject of religion. We contend with its truth claims and account, with empathy or skepticism, for experiences that often fall under the category's description. We do so in light of commitments that define philosophical pragmatism. William James powerfully describes the pragmatist as one who "turns away from abstraction and insufficiency, from verbal solutions, from bad a priori reasons, from fixed principles, closed systems, and pretended absolutes and origins. He turns towards concreteness and adequacy, towards facts, towards action, and towards power. . . . It means the open air and possibilities of nature, as against . . . dogma, artificiality, and the pretense of finality."[1] The good pragmatist then encourages a view of philosophy where the neat conundrums of our professional practice give way to a certain kind of responsibility in our intellectual lives, where we take the tools of our training and work to offer insight, however limited, into specific conditions of value and into the specific consequences of ideas.

On this view, philosophy becomes, as John Dewey argued, "criticism of the influential beliefs that underlie culture; a criticism which traces the beliefs to their generating conditions as far as may be, which tracks them to their results, which considers the mutual compatibility of the elements of the total structure of beliefs." "Such an examination," he goes on to say, "terminates, whether so intended or not, in a projection of them into a new perspective which leads to new surveys of possibilities."[2]

Pragmatists accent an open, malleable, and pluralistic universe, a view in which change is a central feature of our living, demanding of us variety, imagination, and experimentation in practical matters. Richard Rorty might have given us the most radical rendering of what can be called pragmatism's refusal: "the sense that there is nothing deep down inside us except what we have put there ourselves, no criterion that we have not created in the course of creating a practice, no standard of rationality that is not an appeal to such a criterion, no rigorous argumentation that is not obedience to our own conventions."[3] The world is a result of our doing; it is our responsibility and ours alone. Not all pragmatists would agree with everything Rorty says here. But the emphasis on *us*—on what *we* have done and what we *can* do—remains paramount. What follows from pragmatism's refusal, in whatever form, is an insistence that human beings, fragile and fallen though we may be, must bear the responsibility of securing by *practical* means the values we most cherish. From birth we are thrown into the messiness of our living to forge connections and common ground with others apart from abstract transcendental standards. That sense of "thrownness" involves, among other more mundane matters, the fitful task, through deliberation and concerted action with others, of making our world anew when matters break down. The choice that pragmatists make—of accepting the contingent character of starting points and banking our all on the possible—entails accepting our inheritance from, and a deep and abiding relationship and ongoing work with, our fellows as our primary source of guidance.

Obviously such a view can easily place religion in the crosshairs of some pragmatists. From Charles S. Peirce's 1893 essay "Evolutionary Love" to William James's *Varieties of Religious Experience*, John Dewey's *A Common Faith*, Richard Rorty's polytheism, and Cornel West's prophetic pragmatism (a decidedly male affair), pragmatists have sought to think about religion, and it hasn't always turned out well. No matter. Religion remains an important subject for the pragmatist. How could it be otherwise, especially in a country where so many of our fellows have religious commitments? And those commitments animate, directly and indirectly, the social world and often shape political choices.

In my own case, I have tried to think pragmatically about the study of African American religion. Not so much to trouble the category but to take up what the category brings into view and obscures for the scholar. After all, concerns about religion and what it singles out are complicated when we think about it in tandem with race. Whether we use the ethnic moniker of "African American" or the racial designation of "black," the adjective calls attention to the difficult history that colors the way religion is practiced and understood in the United States. The horrors of slavery, the terror of Jim Crow, and the myriad ways in which black people in this country have responded to the absurdity and joy of their conditions of living reveal religion as not only a crucial site for the arduous task of resisting white supremacy but also an important resource in the vexing work of self-creation under captive conditions.

My intention in this chapter is to chart briefly my pragmatic approach to the study of African American religion. This will entail moving between a rather idiosyncratic view of what the phrase singles out (based on a distinction between African American religion and African American religious life) and repeated gestures to what I am calling, in an obvious appropriation of John Dewey, "black religious attitudes"—that is, enduring and deep-seated dispositions tethered to a transformative ideal that all too often fall outside the subject matter of African American religious studies. I try to navigate here a clear tension in my work: that I take seriously African American religion, traditionally understood, while desperately working to think beyond its constraints. As I think and write about both, the social and political context of black life in the United States matters profoundly. From the various forms of expressions of slave religion to the importance of African American Protestantism in the black freedom struggle and to an insistence on black individuality in the face of the dehumanizing practices of white supremacy, pragmatists who ignore or easily dismiss "African American religion" and black religious attitudes, in all of their variations, do so at their peril and, in a way, turn their back on the task of philosophy as I understand it.

In my first book, Exodus!, for example, I wanted to show how African Americans drew on the Exodus story to imagine a sense of peoplehood or racial solidarity and the understanding of mutual obligation that followed from such a view. I aimed to show that racial solidarity rooted in an important Biblical story was not predicated on some essentialist idea of race (after all, the biological view of race had not yet settled into common use in the early part of the nineteenth century) but rather was the result of an ongoing effort to address the problematic of white supremacy and its moral and ethical distortions. I turned to the historical archive to weave a plausible account that troubled contemporary debates about race and expanded how we might understand the role and function of African American religious language in black politics.

My account was not shaped by a priori assumptions about what African American religion is. I was less interested in declaring that African American religion was this-worldly in its orientation and necessarily revolutionary. Nor was I interested in the claim that black religion pacified African Americans and focused their attention on otherworldly matters. Rather, in Exodus!, I tended to the effects of African American religion and the social context of its expression. I wanted to follow the path of the language and see the effects of imagining and acting in this way as opposed to another. By my pragmatic lights, African American religion mattered not because of its truth claims or the unimpeachable authority of the experiences had. African American religion mattered, at least to me, because of "the work" of the practices that fell under the category's description.

I sought to evade the historical encumbrances that have often directed the scholar's attention to a particular set of concerns about African American religion—whether it is a singular preoccupation with black Protestant churches or an overarching concern with theological questions.[4] Instead, following John Dewey, my approach drew and continues to draw on what I call his "inversion strategy," an approach that focuses our attention on the particular organism transacting with her environs in specific ways and in the full light of an ideal that has stirred her to be otherwise. As Dewey writes in A Common Faith, "The actual religious quality in the experience described is the effect produced, the better adjustment in life and its conditions, not the manner and cause of its production. The way in which the experience operated, its function, determines its religious value."[5] He goes on to say: "It is the claim of religions that they effect this generic and enduring change in attitude. I should like to turn the statement around and say that whenever this change takes place there is definitely a religious attitude. It is not a religion that brings it about, but when it occurs, from whatever cause and by whatever means, there is a religious outlook and function."[6] Here Dewey effectively flips the script. We turn away from origins and focus our attention on effects. For him, and I think he is right here, this shift reveals that the "experiences having the force of bringing about a better, deeper, and enduring adjustment in life are not so rare."[7] To my mind this inversion changes how we might study African American religion. It certainly brings a wider range of experiences into view for the scholar, and it does so without necessarily taking on Dewey's rather dismissive claim about the evolutionary diminishment of "old religion" because of some exaggerated view of the ascendance of science.

Take for example an account in Albert Raboteau's classic book *Slave Religion: The "Invisible Institution" in the Antebellum South*. He illustrates the power of the slaves' spiritual agency with the example of Praying Jacob.

> [Praying Jacob] was a slave in the state of Maryland. His Master was very cruel to his slaves. Jacob's rule was to pray three times a day, at just such an hour of the day; no matter what work was or where he might be, he would stop and go and pray. His master has been to him and pointed his gun at him, and told him if he did not cease praying he would blow out his brains. Jacob would finish his prayer and then tell his master to shoot in welcome—your loss will be my gain—I have two masters, one on earth and one in heaven—master Jesus in heaven, and master Saunders on earth. I have a soul and a body; the body belongs to you, master Saunders, and the soul to Jesus.[8]

This account can illustrate the power of supernatural concern: Praying Jacob sees himself as under the protective care of God, and that understanding precipitates a form of rebelliousness. Religion, in this case Jacob's conversion to Methodism, causes a fundamental adjustment in his relation to the world he inhabits. The scholar's attention turns then to the religion that causes this adjustment: to describe it in its details and perhaps attribute to it a political consequence. Conversion, in this instance, stands as an example of the revolutionary potential of slave religion.

But Dewey asks us to shift our attention elsewhere: to the fact that Jacob's religious attitude is evidenced in his disposition toward Master Saunders. The moment Jacob imagines himself in terms that are not those of the slave master, he evidences an adjustment in disposition that is *religious*. Acceptance of a particular teaching can certainly aid in bringing about that adjustment. But to turn our attention to the particulars of his conversion and the theological commitments that come with it throws us into the quagmire of determining what exactly about his conversion experience resulted in the adjustment itself. This is not necessarily a bad thing, but it can generate rather uninteresting debates about the political value of Christianity among slaves. Conversion to Methodism is just one among many experiences that could effect such an outcome.

Imagine the conjurer Sandy empowering Fredrick Douglass to challenge the slave breaker Edward Covey. That encounter in Douglass's *Narrative* resulted in a fundamental adjustment in Douglass that radically changed his orientation to his circumstances and the world. Or take my own personal encounter with Malcolm X's *Autobiography* as a freshman at Morehouse College in Atlanta, Georgia. As a country boy from a small town in Mississippi, I had never encountered a figure like Malcolm X, and the story of his life gave me language to explain my own father's rage, an emotion that had taken residence in me with great tumult. I have never been the same. From whatever cause and by whatever means, the disposition that results, Dewey argues, is what is religious. There has been a fundamental shift in the center of gravity in one's understanding of oneself. An old self has been riven and a new perspective found that emboldens one to *be* differently in the world, and this has political implications—particularly for a people subject to the arbitrary power of those invested in being white.

This approach does not marginalize the traditional subject matter of African American religious studies. It expands it. For me, pragmatism has helped unhinge the field from standard histories that presuppose fixed, static ideas of black identity, that uncritically assert black agency apart from environments that constrain and enable action, and that take for granted a troublesome metaphysics that undergirds struggles against racist practices. The result of the inversion expands the subject matter of African American religious studies, and it calls our attention to a kind of self-fashioning under captive conditions.

The point here is not to deny the significance and substance of religious claims. I don't believe religion should be relegated to some private sphere or that we have advanced in such a way today that we no longer need the "superstitions" of the past to account for the mysteries of our current living. I also do not feel compelled to rethink what theists and those who hold religious commitments are up to when they profess their commitments in public. I take all of this "stuff" seriously. Instead, my aim, at least in part, is to open up space for consideration of those religious attitudes within black America that fall outside of our traditional understanding of African American religion or are simply left out of the dominant story.

||||||||||||||||

Admittedly, I have a particular understanding of African American religion. In *African American Religion: A Very Short Introduction*, I make a distinction between African American religion and African American religious life. Both are shaped by the reality of American racism: the very fact of slavery and its aftermath have affected the form and content of black religious expression in this country. That reality has necessitated the ever-present need to account for one's place in a world, God's world, in which white people are valued more than others. (Theodicy, or the problem of evil, takes on a particular resonance here. Think of W. E. B. Du Bois's searing question: "Why did God make me an outcast and a stranger in mine own house?") It is in this context, at least for me, that African American religion takes on added significance for the scholar.

But we should be clear that African American religious life, as is the case of black life generally, is not reducible to the bare-boned facts of white supremacy. That life contains within it avenues for solace and comfort in God, fortifying and enduring ritual practices that enable a sense of communion with others, answers to questions about who we take ourselves to be and about our relation to mystery or the unknown. Obedience to creed and dogma matter here, and meaning, beyond the ugliness of white people, is often found, for some, in submission to God. In short, African American religious life is as rich and as complicated as the religious life of other groups in the United States. But to my mind, "African American religion" refers to something more specific.

The social and political context in the United States, one animated by the value gap, shapes and informs the study of African American religion and its social place and function. As I argue elsewhere, if the phrase "African American religion" is to have any descriptive usefulness at all, it must signify something *more* than "African Americans who are religious." We know, for example, that African Americans practice a number of different religions. We have black people who are Buddhists, some who are Mor-

mons, and others who are Jehovah's Witnesses. But we rarely, if ever, re-
fer to any of these as examples of African American religion. We don't use
the phrase "black Buddhism," for example.

African American religion calls our attention to something more substantive and specific. I do not mean that the phrase singles out something distinct in experience or something like a religious consciousness
that stands apart from social and historical forces. I don't have Schleier-
macher's hangover. Instead, and I admit this is a bit idiosyncratic, African American religion refers to a racialized reality within which religious
meanings, however understood, have been produced and reproduced.
The history of slavery and racial discrimination in the United States
birthed particular religious formations among African Americans. African Americans converted to Christianity, for example, in the context of
slavery. Many left predominantly white denominations to form their own
after experiencing profound racial humiliation in white churches (e.g.,
"nigger pews," segregated church cemeteries). Some embraced a distinctive interpretation of Islam to make sense of their condition in the United
States. Given that history, we can reasonably and accurately describe certain variants of Christianity and Islam as African American and mean
something beyond the rather uninteresting claim that black individuals
belong to these different religious traditions.

It is also in this context that we see the different effects and outcomes
of various African American adjustments to the reality of racism in this
country—adjustments that resulted in a fundamental and deep-seated
shift in the seat of the self of those who experienced it. In *A Common Faith*,
Dewey distinguishes between "accommodation," "adaptation," and "adjustment." We often use the words interchangeably, but Dewey insists
different attitudes follow from each of these orientations to the social
world. Accommodation is primarily passive—a kind of "fatalistic resig-
nation or submission" to the world as it is. Adaptation is a bit more active. Here we actively modify conditions in accordance to our wants and
purposes. Adjustment is much more significant and enduring. As Dewey
writes, "There are . . . changes in ourselves in relation to the world in
which we live that are more inclusive and deep seated. They relate not to
this and that want in relation to this and that condition of our surround-
ings, but pertain to our being in its entirety. Because of their scope, this

modification of ourselves is enduring."[9] Adjustment is lasting in its implication and not subject to whim. It reflects a fundamental change of will that encompasses the entirety of the life lived from that moment forward.

That kind of adjustment in the context of a racist society, which denies black people standing and often renders them nonpersons, could easily get one killed. And there are numerous examples, known and unknown, of the deadly costs of such an adjustment. Nevertheless it happened. And that fact, at least for me, registers something critically important for the scholar of African American religion: that certain acts of black self-fashioning (heroic efforts at self-creation that were deep seated and enduring) illustrate a "black religious attitude" (and both adjectives are doing work here). In some cases that attitude drew on traditional religious language, and in others the adjustment actively resisted the languages altogether.

In his 1903 classic *The Souls of Black Folk*, W. E. B. Du Bois describes the challenges of self-formation in a society based on the value gap. For him, the strange experience of being a problem typically generated a response among African Americans that ranged from accommodation to what he describes and commends as self-realization. When the young white girl in the New England schoolhouse "refused [his visiting card] peremptorily, with a glance," Du Bois responded by desiring to best white people in all of what they valued. He insisted on a particular view of himself and of his ambition despite what the world said about him and how that relegated him to a narrow corner of the world. But Du Bois also acknowledged:

> With other boys the strife was not so fiercely sunny: their youth shrunk into tasteless sycophancy, or into silent hatred of the pale world about them and mocking distrust of everything white; or wasted itself in a bitter cry, Why did God make me an outcast and a stranger in mine own house. The shades of the prison house closed round about us all: walls straight and stubborn to the whitest, but relentlessly narrow, tall, and unscalable to sons of night who must plod darkly on in resignation.[10]

Here accommodation and adaptation were the primary responses of those bearing the brunt of the value gap. This very personal, intimate reaction becomes the basis for Du Bois's more general account of black leadership and social life. In "Of Mr. Booker T. Washington and Others," he writes: "When to earth and brute is added an environment of men and ideas, then the attitude of the imprisoned group may take three main forms,—a feeling of revolt and revenge; an attempt to adjust all thought and action to the will of the greater group; or, finally, a determined effort at self-realization and self-development despite environing opinion."[11] Adaptation and accommodation define a certain political stance, as exemplified in Booker T. Washington's accommodation to the racist dictates of the South. But Du Bois commends self-realization, a fundamental adjustment in who we take ourselves to be that shifts our orientation to the world because it reflects a deep-seated transformation in our view of ourselves. Such an adjustment exemplifies a black religious attitude.

The words "black" or "African American" work here as markers of difference. They signify a tradition of struggle against white supremacy and a cultural repertoire that reflects that unique journey. When I use the phrase "African American religion" or "black religious attitude," then, I am not referring to something that can be defined substantively apart from the thicket of varied practices; rather, my aim is to orient you in a particular way to the material under consideration, to call attention to a sociopolitical history that informs the topic at hand, and to single out the workings of *imagination* and *faith* under particular conditions.

Sentences that begin with "African American religion is . . ." are rarely simply descriptive. They typically convey certain normative assumptions about what that religion is, has been, and ought to be, like "African American religion is prophetic" or "African American religion is emotional." But to understand the phrase "African American religion is . . ." only in this way risks the problem of reifying a particular understanding of black religious practices (of denying complexity, ambiguity, and contradiction by snatching varied practices out of the messiness of history). It is much better to understand such utterances as a way of saying that you ought to give more attention to *this* as opposed to *that*, and as a recollection of history that makes the distinction worthwhile.

When Howard Thurman, the great twentieth-century black theologian, declared that slaves dared to redeem the religion profaned in their midst, he offered a particular understanding of black Christianity: this expression of Christianity was not the idolatrous embrace of Christian doctrine that justified the superiority of white people and the subordination of black people. Instead, black Christianity embraced the liberating power of Jesus's example: his sense that all, no matter their station in life, were children of God. Thurman sought to orient the reader to a specific inflection of Christianity in the hands of those who lived as slaves. For him and for me, that difference made a difference. We need only listen to the spirituals and give attention to the way African Americans interpreted the gospel, to how they invoked Jesus in their lives. This approach brings into view the particular circumstances that cast Christianity in this way as opposed to that.

That difference is also evidenced in the religious attitude that comes with this unique embrace: that what occurred was not simply a change in will in relation to a particular problem or a distinctive form of Christianity, but rather "a change of will conceived as the organic plenitude of our being."[12] This effect was (and is) made clear in the very way the experience had oriented the person to the society within which she or he lived. No longer content or resigned to accept the assigned terms of her or his birth, she or he dared to be otherwise, with all the risks that entailed. Fannie Lou Hamer comes to mind here: a Mississippi sharecropper who knew only the toil of the cotton fields and the constraints of one of the worst Jim Crow states in the Union imagined herself in terms that enabled her to stand up to her brutal conditions of living. Imagination and faith enabled an envisioning of the self and the world that had profound implications for the particular life lived.

Imagination allowed Hamer to see beyond the opacity of her condition and to grab hold of a transformative ideal that had the power to stir deeply. As Steven Fesmire put it, "Imagination in Dewey's sense is the capacity to concretely perceive what is before us in light of what could be."[13] This imaginative work is intimately bound up with faith, the readiness, as William James wrote, "to act in a cause the prosperous issue of which is not certified in us in advance."[14] It is a faith in the possibilities of who we can become in spite of the brutality of slavery, the terror of Jim Crow, and the ongoing devaluation of black life in this country.

The words "black" or "African American" work, then, as part of a procedure of differentiation and invocation that bring this black religious attitude into full view. Such sentences as "he is saved" or "she is woke" are efforts to point our attention to dispositions that are enduring and deep seated and that come to be known to others in the very way the persons stand in relation to the world as it is and as it could be. (Think, for example, of the moment of Pentecost, not so much to account for the presence of the Holy Spirit but to note the dispositions witnessed by others. Something dramatic happened. And the description speaks volumes: "*they must be drunk.*"[15])

||||||||||||||||||

Any study of African American religion must begin with the claim that the particular and dynamic circumstances of African American life constituted the soil for black religious imaginings. Those imaginings ranged from belief in God and his active role in history (that is, a distinctive theological voice) to an insistence that all is not settled, which provided the opening for imaginative leaps beyond the immediate horrors of life and thereby paved the way for a robust self-imagining in spite of the active work of being thrown into a world defined by the value gap.

In this sense "African American religion" is much more than a description of the religions African Americans practice. The phrase, as I have argued, helps us differentiate a particular set of religious practices from others that are invested in whiteness; it invokes a cultural inheritance that marks the unique journey of African Americans in the United States. African American religion says to those who will listen, pay attention to this as opposed to that—and the distinction is rooted in the sociopolitical realities that shape the experiences of black people in this country.

But none of this is static or fixed. Material conditions shift. Old ideologies die. New ones emerge. In some ways the African American sociologist E. Franklin Frazier was right. He noted in his 1963 classic book, *The Negro Church in America*, that demographic shifts, dramatic changes in labor patterns, and class stratification within African American communities would change the role and function of black churches. The same holds today for how we understand African American religion. Dramatic changes in the nature of work, demographic shifts that involve increased ethnic diversity within black communities, and deepening class stratification have greatly affected the ways we describe African American religion today.

"African American religion," ideally, takes us to particular practices under specific conditions. It is a keyword in our efforts to offer a thick account of a particular moral inheritance. As conditions shift and change, words and phrases that were once helpful in orienting us to certain practices often fall out of use, and new ones emerge as better descriptions. This is not to suggest that the distinctiveness of African American religious life has been lost. That life remains vibrant and complex. But the fear of loss all too often motivates us, particularly scholars, to hang on to outmoded descriptions and blinds us to what is actually going on in the lives of black people in this country.

How we talk about African American religious life, how we account for the myriad ways in which a diverse, racialized group gives expression to their religious beliefs within institutions that constitute a kind of cultural inheritance, may require a different language in a moment of celebrity preachers, Twitter, and Donald Trump. Something has changed. Maybe this is what E. Franklin Frazier was reaching for. The issue in his much-maligned view was not so much that institutions and cultural languages created under one set of conditions faded from view as African Americans were more fully integrated into American society. Instead, new languages had to emerge to describe and account for black life under the shifting conditions of late capitalism and the evolving status of race in the United States.

In the end, three key ideas form the core of my pragmatic approach to the study of African American religion. First, African American religion should be viewed as a distinctive *practice of freedom*. Here black religious imagination is used in the service of opening up spaces closed down by white supremacy. The political nature of that opening varies. It is not necessarily progressive or conservative. Rather, religion becomes a site for self-creation and for communal advancement with political consequences. This view requires situating African American religion within the broader dynamic of African American history. Second, African American religion should be understood as a *sign of difference*. The phrase differentiates particular religious practices from others by reference to specific historical and social contexts that give them shape. African American religion explicitly rejects, as best as possible, the idolatry of white supremacy by proclaiming itself, in practice, as different. And, third, African American religion insists on its *open-endedness*. It offers resources for African

Americans to imagine themselves beyond the constraints of now. This belief that "all is not settled" enables broad leaps of faith that deepen aspirational claims for freedom.

Taken together, these three ideas help the pragmatist navigate the complex and dynamic religious history of African Americans in the United States. They anchor the kinds of stories we write that say something specific about what it might mean to be black and to hold religious views in a country that is simultaneously democratic, predominantly Christian, and profoundly racist. These ideas also guide our attention to the heroic efforts of black people in this country to imagine themselves anew under captive conditions and to express a faith that they could, in fact, do so despite what the world arbitrarily does to them. In this sense, the phrase "African American religion" turns our attention to a wonderfully human response to the ongoing ordeal of living.

What is required of the scholar of African American religion is a thick description of the practices that fall under that category. If the category of African American religion helps us in doing that work, then it remains useful. If the phrase is an outmoded description that blocks the way to a fuller understanding of the complex responses among black people to the realities of race in the United States, then it is time we got rid of it. In either case, a richer and more complex historical story of the practices the phrase singles out is required, one that doesn't fix our eyes in one direction. I turn to this issue in the next chapter.

El Anatsui, *Omen*, 1978, ceramic and manganese,
15½ × 21 × 16½ inches. © El Anatusi, Courtesy of the artist and
Jack Shainman Gallery, New York.

Babel in the North

Black Migration, Moral Community, and
the Ethics of Racial Authenticity

In the previous chapter I suggested that any account of the study of African American religion must take seriously the historical and sociopolitical context of African American life. In fact, context gives African American religion its distinctive meaning. The phrase "African American religion" orients the scholar in a specific way to experiences often deemed religious and sets those experiences apart from others in the full light of the realities of race that have shaped (and continue to shape) the United States and the lives of black people who live here.

How scholars attend to that context and write the histories of African American religion matters. Our particular orientation to evidence and our narrative choices guide the attention of the reader. These choices bring certain events, characters, and conflicts into view while obscuring others. For example, a singular focus on churches, male preachers, or denominations blocks from view other social spaces and actors (e.g., black popular culture, black literary production, gendered work spaces, etc.) within African American religious life. It most certainly blinds us to black religious attitudes as an object of study. We see only that which our limited accounts and stories want us to see.

Writing African American religious history is not simply a dispassionate detailing of facts. We aren't chroniclers. Instead, we actively shape the stories we tell, developing certain characters and events, with particular purposes and interests in mind. Although I don't have the space to explore the nuances of my view here, I want to suggest that histories of African American religion involve a choice of plot structure for sequences of events. As Hayden White notes, "The 'story' which the historian purports to 'find' in the historical record is proleptic to the 'plot' by which the events are finally revealed to figure a recognizable structure of relationships of a specifically mythic sort."[1] The historian is doing *active* work.

In writing such histories, we find ourselves negotiating the authority of tradition, the constraining power of conventions, and encountering the limits of narrative form. We emplot. We choose paradigms of explanation, and we repeatedly make moral or ideological decisions along the way. Histories of African American religion, then, are always written, even when not explicitly acknowledged to be so, from a self-consciously critical point of view and in full awareness of the temporal distance between us and the subject(s) about which we write. That distance is often bridged, however, by the overdetermining presence of the value gap that connects the past about which we write with a present within which we live. As such, the historiography of African American religion and its narratives of recovery, redemption, and resistance all too often reflect an ongoing political and existential reality that presses in on the evidence. In this sense, I am in complete agreement with Robert Orsi: "The history of the study of religion is always a political history,"[2] with, I might add, a presentist undertow.

This is especially so for a people caught on the underside of a country committed to democracy *and* the value gap. The history of the study of African American religion is always a political history of sorts. The phrase calls our attention to religious meanings produced in the face of the value gap and its often deadly consequences. But it is the *critical orientation* that draws my attention.[3] The writing of African American religious history carries with it, though not necessarily, political concerns that are tied to ideas of black resistance and freedom, agency and identity. Here Michael Oakeshott's strict separation of the university study of history from actual politics is cast aside. For him, we study history not with an eye to resolve political problems or policy debates in our time or for the lessons gleaned from the past for our current political circumstances. Instead, Oakeshott insisted that historians concern themselves with elucidating an "impractical past," one that isn't overdetermined by the problems of our day.[4] To my mind, this is an odd demand and constraint for a people often found on the bottom of History's foot.

Oakeshott recognized that this kind of writing was a tall order. He wrote,

> The historical past is always present; and yet historical experience is always in the form of the past. And this contradiction must remain unresolved so long as we remain within the world of historical ideas. History, because it is experience, is present, its facts are present facts, its world a present world of ideas; but because it is history, the formulation of experience as a whole as *sub specie praeteritorum*, it is the continuous assertion of a past which is not past and of a present which is not present.[5]

But Oakeshott's complex view of history reeks of someone secure in the comforts of an elite and decidedly white university space and locked away from the deadly consequences of practical politics. He would certainly frown upon Frantz Fanon's insistence that, because of the enduring legacy of white supremacy and colonialism, history could not be other than a critical battleground for those who have borne the brunt of the West's conceit.

It is in this light that writing the history of African American religion takes on such significance. The archive is mobilized, by some, to help the reader to think and, by extension, act differently. And our stories do this work by exposing hidden presuppositions and foregrounding different characters and events that unsettle settled accounts of what was and what is.

As a pragmatist, I prefer George Herbert Mead's approach to history. Mead understood the past as a condition of the present—without it we lose our temporal bearing in the moment we occupy by cutting ourselves off from funded experiences that aid in the navigation of our current circumstances. Practical matters can never be simply quarantined. We understand where we are, the things we care about, and the current lives we live in light of the "doings and sufferings" of others who came before us. But for Mead, there are moments in the present—the emergence of novelty—that do not follow from the past, or as he put it, a moment in which "the past relative to which it was novel cannot be made to contain it."[6] In other words, its newness is seen in relation to our past experiences, but those experiences themselves cannot help account for the newness itself (it's unlike anything we've ever experienced before). For the present, there is always a past. And in those moments when true novelty emerges and our current story cannot account for it, we must tell ourselves a story that, in fact, will. For Mead, *the past will vary as the present varies.*

This not only obtains for accounting for novelty but also shapes our ongoing efforts to disrupt invocations of the past that justify current social, political, and economic arrangements, and blocks the way for the full blossoming of the new. We turn to the archive, as Theodor Adorno insisted, to "open thinking points beyond itself,"[7] to reveal hidden presuppositions that guide our attention in one direction as opposed to another, and to expose operations (particularly the operations of power) that legitimate the current order of things. In this sense, *a critical pragmatic approach to history* insists on offering accounts that shift the center of gravity of how we understand ourselves and the world we inhabit. It rejects attempts to map timeless patterns of human conduct by writing a different story of how some problematics come to occupy our attention and why some ought to be left aside. What determines the path of such an account has everything to do with the present problematic we face.

For the pragmatist, the active work of historians is always shaped by the demands and constraints of the present context under which they write. And it is here, for those of us who take up history as a critical enterprise (and I am not arguing that one *must* do this), that our narrative choices and the politics that inform them matter most. In the writing of African American religious history, we have often been unduly bound to historical accounts that aim to reveal black agency as resistance or we have too often been tied to histories of decline and progress that narrow the range of our objects of study. I believe we need to reach for a different kind of politics and a different historical story, one that opens our thinking about what the phrase "African American religion" might single out, casts aside old, worn binaries rooted in a singular focus on black Protestantism, and urges the reader to think and, perhaps, act differently. In what follows, I focus my attention on a once standard account of African American religion and the interwar period to gesture at how we might write such a history.

|||||||||||||||||

Traditional historical accounts of African American religious life in the 1920s and 1930s often describe mainline black churches as unable to cope with the pressures of urbanization that coincide with the Great Migration. The period has been described as the "era of sects and cults"—the moment in which we see the proliferation of storefront churches and the emergence of esoteric cults and charismatic leaders with peculiar theologies. The emergence of these groups is often attributed to a psychological dislocation that occurred in the shift from rural to urban life as well as to the failure of traditional religious languages to account for the migrants' new circumstances. As this particular story goes, black southern migrants—with the push factors of southern racial violence and agricultural disaster and the pull factors of the promise of a better life in the North—found themselves adrift in industrial urban America. The so-called cults and storefronts provided them with a ballast and an anchor.

The rising presence of storefronts and so-called cults in urban black America signaled a decline among traditional black churches or what Gayraud Wilmore goes as far as to call the "deradicalization of the Black Church." In Wilmore's view, at least three significant factors hampered the ability of mainline black denominations to maintain their historic roles as the central institution in the public and private lives of African Americans. First, many congregations lacked the financial resources and an adequately trained ministry to affect any significant influence on their respective communities. The impoverished churches also retained what Wilmore calls a rural orientation. They relied on a moralistic and revivalistic interpretation of Christianity to hold off the pain and miseries of their lives. This particular approach led to a passive relation to the actual political challenges that short-circuited the possibility of a better life.

Second, the proliferation of black churches throughout the cities weakened the overall impact of black religion by diffusing its economic and political potential. According to Wilmore, this resulted in competitive denominationalism and rivalries among congregations that "diverted energies and money from self-help and community welfare concerns to ecclesiastical gamesmanship and institutional housekeeping."[8] These realities were only compounded by the increased competition mainline churches encountered from secular organizations.

The third factor points to the growth of black civil society beyond the institutional boundaries of the churches. Social clubs, fraternities, lodges, and other small private groups began to take on roles that were increasingly beyond the reach of the church and its doctrine. And for Wilmore, this signaled an important shift: "The church, which throughout most of the nineteenth century was able to integrate much of the activity of the masses around the core of its own ideology of racial uplift and moral development, now found itself relegated to the periphery of the closed circle that was the segregated black community. From that eccentric and unfamiliar position the church began to offer personal security for older adults—mostly female—of the lower middle class."[9] The marginal status of mainline black churches was solidified as the profane dimensions of black life associated with a "debased" class of the black poor and an emergent, confident, and somewhat secular black intelligentsia began to take center stage. In short, Wilmore would have us believe that between an expanding black underclass and a rising black middle class, black churches lost their leading role in black communities throughout the urban North.

A melodramatic story. Recent work has troubled this account. We need only read Barbara Savage's *Your Spirit Walks Beside Us: The Politics of Black Religion*, Wallace Best's *Passionately Human, No Less Divine: Religion and Culture in Black Chicago, 1915–1952*, and Judith Weisenfeld's *New World A-Coming: Black Religion and Racial Identity during the Great Migration* to get a more complex picture of the period. The narrative of the rise of so-called sects and cults and the decline of black churches in the North requires exaggerated conflicts and disfigured characters to make sense. The historical record suggests that black churches bore the brunt of the responsibility for the new migrant population. Traditional churches experienced unprecedented growth in their memberships due to the migration of black southerners. Albert Tindley's East Calvary Methodist Episcopal Church in Philadelphia, for example, saw its active membership increase to over 7,000 persons by 1923, and the membership of Ebenezer Baptist Church in Pittsburgh grew from 1,500 members to close to 3,000 between 1915 and 1926.[10]

In fact, a careful look at the *Census of Religious Bodies* for the years 1926 and 1936 "points to a 9 percent increase in all black membership among all denominations, from 5.2 million to 5.7 million." Black Baptists showed the most remarkable increase, growing "from 3.2 million in 1926 to nearly 3.8 million a decade later."[11] Even if we account for the great deal of turnover among members as well as the deliberate exaggeration of church roles, the Great Migration era remains an extraordinary time of growth for traditional black churches in the North.[12] To be sure, churches confronted tremendous challenges, but to characterize their efforts as a retreat or, even worse, as an indication of deradicalization is to succumb to a melodramatic *narrative of decline*. And for Wilmore, the choice of this plot structure aims for a certain kind of epiphany: that the reader will see the necessity of a particular black theological project to reclaim the "high" moment of the church lost during the interwar period. This is the moral decision that is made (proleptic to the plot) and, perhaps, one of the main problems of the narrative.

This story of decline presupposes a number of different ideas. First, it assumes that there is a high moment in black church history, usually the church of the nineteenth century, when black religious institutions served the spiritual and social needs of black communities. Second, it assumes a fixed view of what constitutes the social and political role of the church, often drawing a hard distinction between an otherworldly theological orientation (the bad view) and one that is based in a this-worldly social ethic (the good view). And finally, implicit and sometimes explicit in each of these assumptions is an understanding of what the *true* theology of the black church is. This view serves as the basis to judge the relative effectiveness of black religious institutions. In the end, the plot is that once upon a time the church was central to black folks' lives, but in the 1920s and 1930s it was not. There was a tragic descent. I want to pick out two central themes here that will hopefully get at some of the trouble with this interpretation and use them to offer a different way of making sense of this critical moment in the religious and political life of black America.

|||||||||||||||||||

The emergence of diverse black religious expression in the 1920s and 1930s is often accounted for in the narrative of decline as an indication of (1) the fading moral significance of traditional black churches and (2) the eclipse of moral ends these institutions embody. The former speaks to processes of secularization, in the familiar way we understand the term, that turn otherwise faithful individuals into unfaithful people or, minimally, privately faithful people. On this view, the Great Migration unleashed torrid forces that led to the differentiation and stratification of black life, accelerated black civil society's late nineteenth-century emergence as an independent sphere, and made possible other domains of living that influenced the moral character of black individuals. A concern, then, about the disenchantment of black life and a subsequent loss of meaning for African Americans animates this particular view.

The influx of black southern migrants dramatically affected religious life in northern black communities. By 1926 Harlem alone contained more than 140 churches. In addition to traditional mainline black churches, nontraditional forms of black religious expression emerged with groups that exhibited what Judith Weisenfeld calls distinctive "religio-racial identities." Because of this diversity and plurality, according to the narrative of decline, the moral significance of black religious life began to fade. In particular, the emergence of storefronts and nontraditional forms of black religious expression, like the Moorish Science Temple or the Nation of Islam, led to the church's loss of its broader purpose and resulted in a narrow focus on its own individual aggrandizement. The institution that once provided the black community with moral and political languages to challenge the state had now been relegated to "ecclesiastical gamesmanship and institutional housekeeping."[13]

The fading moral significance of black churches is directly connected to the eclipse of moral ends these institutions supposedly embody. For some, the diversity of black religious expression led to navel-gazing among individual religious institutions. Preachers were concerned only with the spiritual well-being of their members. An otherworldly focus dominated the theological orientation of the church. Miles Mark Fisher, for example, believed that the otherworldly focus of the church prevented many from seeing the social, political, and economic forces negatively transforming the lives of its membership. Instead, preachers "invoked the Bible as the solution to social problems. Biblical literalism and theological fundamentalism proved the order of the day."[14] Commentary on the structural forces impacting the lives of black Christians was relatively absent from black sermons; instead, the behavior of individuals in a corruptible world was their primary concern.

Such an outlook is directly connected to the notion that the "real" social aims of black religious institutions were lost to the individual desires of those caught in the enticing lights of urban America. Just as the influx of southern migrants diversified the religious landscape of black urban enclaves, the impact of industrialization, greater mobility, and secularization turned these migrants away from the traditional church *and* blinded the traditional church to the *true* meaning of its theology. The lure of the street and the rational pursuit with maximum efficiency of newfound desires became the measure of success. And the church, finding itself on the margins of this new instrumental reason, sought to offer otherworldly salvation (metaphysical security) to its membership.

To my mind, the basic thrust of the story rests on a confusion about how best to describe the evolution of the black church from a nineteenth-century institution to a twentieth-century one. On the one hand, there is the notion that black religious institutions lacked the capacity to handle the influx of black southern migrants. This fact combined with the eroding effects of urbanization and secularization displaced the black church as the central institution in the lives of black Americans *and* obscured the so-called true meaning of its theology. On the other hand, black churches are characterized as otherworldly and theologically conservative. Such an orientation prevented black religious institutions from intervening meaningfully in the lives of black individuals as the forces of urbanization and industrialization transformed their environs.

In the first view, the primary causes of the decline are nonmoral: the decline is a negative byproduct of social change. Black religious institutions simply responded inadequately to change. The second view, however, criticizes the theological orientation of black churches: these churches were doomed to fail because they maintained an otherworldly focus, which turned their attention away from the material forces changing the circumstances of their members' lives. The primary cause of decline is a moral lapse, in the sense that the motivations that actuate black religious folk are connected to certain moral ideals about how we ought to orient ourselves to the world and others. This orientation failed in the face of modernizing forces but was not a consequence of them.

No matter how the story is structured, though, the conclusions appear to be basically the same: that "a relative quietism and an apparent vacuum of church leadership" best characterizes the state of mainstream black religion during this period.[15] I think these conclusions are wrong for a number of reasons (primarily because of standing assumptions that block from view the complexity of African American religious life). But I do acknowledge the importance of key features in narratives of decline. We do have to account for the consequences of urbanization and industrialization, the proliferation of religious forms (traditional and nontraditional) throughout black urban centers, and the potential effects of these events on the form and content of African American religious and political life. The language of decline, however, gets in the way. Attention ought to be given, instead, to the *transformation* of a particular moral community and the moral languages that animate it under shifting material conditions. With this shift in focus, a different story with different actors comes into fuller view.

IIIIIIIIIIIIIIII

In *Ethics after Babel: The Language of Morals and Their Discontents*, Jeffrey Stout argues that the task of the moral philosopher does not begin with unearthing foundational principles that allow us to say, once and for all, what constitutes *the* moral language that we all use. Nor is the task simply to look at major historical actors whose redescriptions have impacted the way we see and talk about ourselves and the world around us. Instead, moral philosophy ought to be understood as a kind of *reflexive ethnography*. It requires of us attention to the intricate details of our moral languages and the forces that can lead to adjustments, transformations, and even wholesale abandonment of words that comprise our moral discourse.

With the emergence of new social practices and institutions, distinctions that once helped us make sense of events may become difficult to manage, and this can lead to all sorts of problems as our moral language falls out of step with new circumstances. The black migrants of the 1920s and 1930s, for example, had a moral language in hand when they arrived in the North. This language developed in a particular social, political, and economic milieu in which certain kinds of distinctions made sense. The context of the Jim Crow South constrained certain kinds of actions, particularly an exhibition of an open disregard for the social mores that undergirded racial segregation. But it does not follow that accommodation to Jim Crow necessarily entailed an internal acceptance of the system of oppression. The internal attitudes of black southerners must be distinguished from their external actions. Otherwise, we would have to account for the civil rights movement as a kind of spontaneous expression of freedom dreams without precedent. Black cultural and political life, and the languages that attend both, existed within and apart from the disciplinary practice of de jure segregation.

A culture of dissemblance, the importance of communal life ranging from organized churches and lodges to informal modes of socializing (practices often beyond the gaze of white folks), or simply a belief in the love of God enabled individuals living in the Jim Crow South to understand themselves apart from their conditions of living. Each provided them with the recognition required to see themselves as self-determining agents in spite of the brutal realities of systemic segregation. However, in a northern urban context these very modes of being, and the languages that go along with them, could easily prove ill-fitted to new sets of problems. A moral language developed within the context of one set of economic, social, and political constraints may be carried over into another context in which technology, social arrangements, modes of production, and political realities (de facto segregation) are quite different. In such circumstances the language may fail to provide appropriate or feasible guidance.

Descriptions of these processes as a decline or as indicative of the deradicalization of traditional black churches will not get us very far in understanding the significance and outcomes of the changes. Such an approach has led to a search for a more pristine expression of what some take to be the moral language of the black church and, by extension, African American communities. For the pragmatist, there is no predetermined, uniform, and unchanging moral language—one that always has the right words and advice for us—that stands apart from our particular situations and problems. Reflections on African American religion or, more specifically, on the black church "can claim no uniform or unchanging subject matter." Changes in our form of life too often yield new ways of living that we did not anticipate and offer up ways for us to be new kinds of people.[16] The dramatic changes in African American religious life during the 1920s and 1930s illustrate such a rich moment in which unanticipated ways of living in the world and new black characters, such as the "New Negro," the Garveyite, and the black communist, emerged in the face of transforming social forces and blurred inherited distinctions.

With the plurality and diversity of African American religious life in the urban North, certain notions commonsensically understood by all could no longer be taken for granted when black persons with different religious commitments engaged one another about their conditions of living. Perhaps I can make the point clearer with the following thought experiment. Imagine a conversation between three black people; each professes a belief in God and that belief serves as the basis for their public actions. Let's say that one of the individuals is a recent migrant from the rural South and is Baptist. Another embraces the social gospel and was born in the North, and the other is a member of a storefront Pentecostal church. All of them ascribe ultimate authority to God, and their opinions about the state of black America are intimately connected to that authority. Suppose also that each of them is familiar with the views of the other. The Baptist and Pentecostal know that the advocate of the social gospel has criticized their theology as otherworldly. He has even gone as far as to suggest that persons with such views have turned their backs on the true message of Christ. The proponent of the social gospel knows that the Pentecostal sees himself as reclaiming the true spirit of Christianity and that he believes his style of worship to be the best way of expressing that spirit. He also knows that the rural Baptist is firmly committed to his views because they have carried him out of the South. It does not follow that it will make much sense for each of them to appeal to the authority of God or scripture in settling disputed questions in public about the state of black America.

Of course, many people did settle disputes this way in the 1920s and 1930s. They talked about moral vices like drinking, gambling, and crime. But they were distinctly *religious persons*. In terms of a general public discussion about the problems of black America, many *individuals with religious conviction* understood that others with similar concerns about the state of black America held incompatible (not necessarily incommensurable) views of what God and the Bible said about the political condition of black people in the United States. So, given the diversity of belief *and* the awareness of that diversity, it would be unwise for any of the three interlocutors to appeal to their religious beliefs in an effort to convince the other about what would be an appropriate course of political action for black people. The underlying interest in upending white supremacy, however, may get them to avoid invoking their religious beliefs as a basis for their political activity; it may get them "arguing in new ways, putting new twists on familiar usages and possibly even bringing new candidates for truth and falsehood into being without trying to do so."[17]

The point here is that the plurality and diversity of black religious life in the 1920s and 1930s contributed significantly to the transformation of black moral discourse or, even better, contributed to the secularization of black public discourse in the North.

I do not mean by secularization that process by which faithful people are made unfaithful or "the passage, transfer, or relocation of those persons, things, functions, meanings, and so forth, from their traditional location in the religious sphere to the secular spheres."[18] Rather, I maintain that the secularization of discourse in black public settings reflects the inability of those who hold theological commitments, who nonetheless wish to speak to a religiously plural audience, to take for granted that others are presupposing the same commitments they are.[19] I am not suggesting that religiosity among black individuals waned or that mainline black churches somehow lost their importance in black communities. Instead, I am arguing that perhaps traditional religious presuppositions that informed African American public life in the nineteenth century could no longer be taken for granted in the twentieth century. The religious convictions of nontraditional forms of black religious expression, the theology of some churches, and the emergence of black public institutions that stood apart from black churches contributed to the secularization of black public discourse. It is a mistake, I believe, to attribute the effects of this secularization to a failure on the part of mainline black denominations to address the spiritual and social needs of their communities. The story is much more complicated than that.

The effort to deliberate across the plurality and diversity of black religious life and address the circumstances of black folk in urban America spurred the secularization of black public discourse in the urban North. The underlying agreement of the need for critical reflection on the circumstances of African Americans remained. A moral language was simply needed to negotiate the plurality and diversity of belief among African Americans, particularly when, as Hubert Harrison, the founder of the short-lived Liberty League, noted, black radicals ranged from "agnostics, atheists, I.W.W.'s Socialists, Single Taxers and even Bolshevists."[20] The change in what these individuals could presuppose and the subsequent effort to accommodate that change had a great effect on the form and content of black moral discourse. It contributed to what can be called an *ethics of racial authenticity*.

|||||||||||||||||||

The ethics of racial authenticity find their starting point in a basic lesson learned from black Christianity: that black folk are a unique people with a different moral sense about them, capable of distinguishing intuitively the wrongness of slavery and racial discrimination and the rightness of their common complaint because of their distinctive relationship to God. This connection with God allows them to step outside of the master-slave relationship, which defines the slave as a means to the master's ends, and to see themselves as self-determining agents. Ideally and ironically, this relationship with God made possible, at least in the nineteenth century, a notion of black autonomy.

The ethics of racial authenticity assume the moral thrust of this lesson but with a significant difference. God is no longer required to be in touch with the uniqueness of an individual or the race. Instead, *an expressivist conception of the racial self* takes hold. African Americans are self-determining agents because something is unique about them *as* black people. They are autonomous because their actions are a sole product of their own will. External factors like God's love or recognition by white people do not determine who they are as individuals or as members of the black race. Something inside of black individuals defines their relation to others and themselves. Imitation here becomes a cardinal sin and self-creation a virtue. On the expressivist view, if black individuals fail to connect with this inner something and with those who are similarly situated, they will in effect fail to live the life that is uniquely theirs. Likewise, if black people as a whole fail to embrace their peculiar, unique form of life, then they will in effect fail to live in the way that is truly theirs. Added moral significance and gravity is then given to the idea of being true to oneself and to notions of racial obligation. This belief would be evidenced in enduring and deep-seated dispositions.

Black expressivism is one of the languages that accommodated the changes in black public discourse, a modernist language of racial authenticity that affected, for good or ill, the form and content of black moral discourse in the North well into the twentieth century (even into our present moment).[21] Secularizing forces transformed the role of black religious language in public deliberation. The material conditions of black urban life made certain distinctions about race less clear. Notions of respectability and racial uplift were reconsidered or at least recalibrated to address the problems of this new black public. And this effort reflected the increased plurality and diversity, precipitated by domestic and international migration, of black urban living in the North. Black religious language continued to shape black public utterances, but it no longer (if it ever did) formed the background agreement within which notions of right and wrong, social activism, and the individual well-being of African Americans could be made intelligible in the urban North.

Structural changes in the setting and the diversity and plurality of black life affected that role significantly. Marcus Garvey, for example, recognized this shift. An article in the *Negro World* in 1923 offered the language of his Universal Negro Improvement Association as an alternative.

> The churches were not doing the work undertaken by Marcus Garvey, yet some preachers are among the crusaders. A full explanation of their attitude might be pretty hard to arrive at and harder to state without entering on contentious matter. It is enough simply to point out the obvious fact that Negro churches are divided, in some cases forbidden to work together with other movements, and they furnish no convenient meeting-ground for united work. Only a movement that welcomes all people of all denominations and is officially attached to none while having its own assembly hall can spread its net wide enough to gather in all people desiring to identify with it.[22]

Garvey's point about a "convenient meeting-ground" must be understood beyond talk of physical buildings. Like many black people in the North, he saw the need for a moral discourse that allowed black folk with varied commitments to reflect together on their circumstances. Religious sectarianism blocked the way. An ethic of racial authenticity offered an alternative path.

Alain Locke, in his manifesto "The New Negro," captured the basic thrust of this shift and the impact it had on the form and content of black moral discourse:

> The Negro to-day wishes to be known for what he is, even his faults and shortcomings, and scorns a craven and precarious survival at the price of seeming to be what he is not. He resents being spoken of as a social ward or minor, even by his own, and to being regarded a chronic patient for the sociological clinic, the sick man of American Democracy. For the same reasons, he himself is through with those social nostrums and panaceas, the so-called solutions of his problem, with which he and the country have been so liberally dosed in the past. Religion, freedom, education, money— in turn, he has ardently hoped for and peculiarly trusted these things; he still believes them, but not in blind trust that they alone will solve his life-problem.[23]

Locke found traditional responses to the problems of black people wanting. Religion and the important tropes of modern liberalism—freedom, education, and money—failed to change substantively the lives of African Americans. In their place or at least as a framework within which these notions could be given deeper significance, Locke offered racial expressivism. He wrote that "each generation . . . will have its creed, and that of the present is the belief in the efficacy of collective effort, in racial cooperation. This *deep feeling of race* is at present the mainspring of Negro life."[24] He goes on to say:

> The deep feeling of race was made possible, on Locke's view, by the extraordinary migration of black people from the South to the North. Up to this point, the idea of racial solidarity was an effect of white racial proscription, an outcome of a common condition among otherwise different individuals. With the influx of black southerners into northern cities, however, Locke saw the emergence of a common black consciousness. "The chief bond between [black folk] has been that of a common condition rather than a life in common. In Harlem, Negro life is seizing upon its first chances for group expression and self-determination."[25] The Great Migration enabled the possibility of an authentic life and art for black people.

Langston Hughes wrote of the new migrants: "They furnish a wealth of colorful, distinctive material because they still hold their own individuality in the face of American standardizations. And perhaps these people will give to the world its truly great Negro artist, the one who is not afraid to be himself."[26]

Josef Sorett brilliantly explores the significance of this kind of thinking in his book *Spirit in the Dark: A Religious History of Black Aesthetics*.

Sentiments such as those of Alain Locke and Langston Hughes were expressed throughout the 1920s and 1930s. We see them in the language of Garveyism and even in the rhetoric of black communists. Garvey's anthropology announced that "man is the individual who is able to shape his own character, master his own will, direct his own life and shape his own needs."[27] He understood that black people, like people in general, were distinctive because of their will, which was the source of their freedom to act and choose. This view gave added weight to their political and cultural ambitions: that despite the many differences, religious and otherwise, that make up the black world, a common sense of who black people are and the shared beliefs that flow from this sense ought to orient them to the world and others.

Garvey was not alone in his political take on the ethics of racial authenticity. Black communists often brought together an expressivist conception of the black self and the ideological program of the Communist Party, finding spaces within the party, as Robin D. G. Kelley demonstrates, "to create an expressive culture which, in some respects, contradicted the movement's goal of interracial solidarity."[28] The black communist William L. Patterson, sounding a lot like Alain Locke, wrote in 1933 that African Americans were connected by a common culture. He said that "the spirituals, the jazz, their religious practices, a growing literature, descriptive of their environment, all of these are forms of cultural expression. . . . Are these not the prerequisites for nationhood?"[29] Strivings for racial authenticity—in the aftermath of World War I and in the context of reconfigured social practices and institutions due to the influx of black migrants—aided in the emergence of a moral language within which a number of different folk with varying political views and quite different religious commitments, if any at all, could talk and reflect on African American life.[30]

Again, this does not mean that black Christianity or, more generally, African American religious life waned. Evelyn Brooks Higginbotham and Lerone Martin have demonstrated quite convincingly that vernacular black church culture thrived during this period, that the popularity of religious race records "gave a new public dimension to black religion and especially to the working-class churches."[31] What Higginbotham calls the "age of the voice" had everything to do with the transformation of the northern religious landscape by southern migrants who challenged traditional forms of religious expression. But the way black individuals in the North talked about their condition with one another certainly changed.[32] People who continued to make appeals to religious beliefs as a basis for settling disputes or conceiving of strategies for public action were simply thought of as *religious folk*, individuals whose public actions were primarily defined by their religious commitments. These were people who "sought to establish boundaries around their lives in the effort to shield them from dangers that were perceived as emanating from both outside and inside their own communities."[33]

But even this heightened activity of black vernacular church culture must be understood in the full light of its place within American capitalism and its effect on black urban life. Black people were now able to purchase gospel blues or recorded sermons and listen to them in the privacy of their own homes or among friends. A new relationship to the content of black religious life was established. Individuals could play the records over and over again. Skip the parts they did not like. Turn the phonograph off when something else caught their attention. The commodification of black religious life simultaneously extended its public appeal—large numbers now had access to black religious culture—and transformed the nature and consumption of that appeal. They were listening to it in commodified form in the privacy of their own homes.

||||||||||||||||||

I have suggested that efforts to accommodate the plurality and diversity of black religious expression in the North contributed significantly to the secularization of black moral discourse, particularly in the way African Americans reflected publicly on their conditions of living. I have offered only a preliminary sketch of the importance of the ethics of racial authenticity in light of these substantive changes, and this serves as a beginning for a more nuanced history of the persistence of racial expressivism in African American politics. Much more work needs to be done. Still in need of refinement is our understanding of the connection between migration, the rise of protest ideologies that shaped this particular moment, and the dispositions that embody the risks taken. The ethics of racial authenticity offer one way of understanding that connection: we see how certain facets of black modernism are intimately connected to changes in the role and function of African American religion in black political life. But the emergence of this moral vocabulary and the way it took hold in the North require thicker descriptions of the way a moral community and its various languages were transformed in the face of extraordinary events. That is difficult to do when predictable plots and stock characters overdetermine how we tell the story.

El Anatsui, *Gbeze*, 1979, manganese,
14¾ × 18 × 15 inches. © El Anatusi, Courtesy of the artist and
Jack Shainman Gallery, New York.

An Uncommon Faith
Rereading W. E. B. Du Bois on Religion

In chapter 1 I suggested, following John Dewey, that philosophy should be thought of as a form of "criticism of the influential beliefs that underlie culture," the aim of which is to open up different pathways for new, and better, possibilities.[1] This view of philosophy develops out of an insistence that we take seriously the context of our beliefs, what Dewey describes as the background and selective interests that bring certain matters into view and leave others aside.

Background refers to "the whole environment of which philosophy must take account in all of its enterprises."[2] Here regulative traditions, those apperceptive organs or mental habits that enable us to get about, are absolutely critical to how we think. In fact, we can't think without them. As Dewey put it, "Surrounding, bathing, saturating the things of which we are explicitly aware is some inclusive situation which does not enter into the direct material of reflection."[3] Only when we have a sense that this background has a bearing on or may even be responsible for some confusion that currently has us hemmed in does it enter in our reflections. Otherwise it remains stable, settled. We turn to context, or at least we ought to turn to context, when we confront problematic situations to better ground our efforts to clear up matters. On this view, "the direct material of every reflection proceeds out of some *precedent* state of affairs in reference to which the existing state is disturbed or problematic to which it is an 'answer' or solution."[4]

Of course, *we* matter in all of this. Selective interest refers to the undeniable role of our individual attitudes, tastes, and biases in the selection of this subject matter as opposed to that. "There is selectivity (and rejection) in every operation of thought," Dewey argued. "There is care, concern implicated in every act of thought. There is someone who has affection for some things over others; when he becomes a thinker he does not leave his characteristic affection behind."[5] When we leave out context—actively ignore background and selective interests—we all too easily slip into what Dewey calls the fallacy of unlimited extension, where we "convert abstraction from a *specific* context into an abstraction from all contexts whatsoever."[6] To avoid this pitfall, we must be attentive to the significant features and outcomes of human doings and sufferings found in traditions and institutions. We must take seriously history and our role in shaping how it comes to us.

This is particularly true of black people caught on the underside of American life. African American history carries the burden of selective interests in the very plot of the story told—one that often highlights the hell of white supremacy and the background of relentless efforts to end its stranglehold. And in most accounts religion has played a central role in that effort. What I tried to do in chapter 2 is upend a particular story about black Christianity that has haunted the field of African American religious studies (and, in the process, illustrate my own pragmatic historicist approach).

A certain account of the decline of black churches during the interwar period reinforces a standard, and rather stale, picture of African American religion—one that fixes our eyes on black churches and their supposedly inadequate theologies and turns us away from the various languages and practices that emerged as a response, in part, to the shifting material conditions of modern black life. Of course, much more needs to be said here. But for my purposes that brief history illustrates two important points: First, African American religious history and how we write it matters insofar as that history orients us to contemporary problems in specific ways; it brings certain problems into view and leaves others in the shadows. Second, more attention needs to be given to the dispositions formed in the crucible of American racism that are, as I see it, illustrative of a black religious attitude.

|||||||||||||||||

Obviously, John Dewey's philosophy and, particularly, *A Common Faith* have shaped my approach to the study of African American religion. Dewey consistently deposits his efforts to reconstruct philosophy in a broad sweeping history of Western ideas. He reveals why some problems that come to us and that reflect a particular period of time are best left to the side. He does something similar with the category of religion. In *A Common Faith*, for example, Dewey puts forward, among other ideas, an evolutionary account of religion: that it emerged under a set of primitive conditions, and as our knowledge and methods of inquiry developed—particularly with the ascendance of science—religion as a mode of explanation was no longer needed. This account underlies his more benevolent attempts to afford those moderns who have embraced science a way to be religious in a decidedly secular world.

Surprisingly, I have always had an ambivalent relation to this little book with big ideas. Not because I disagree with the argument (although I reject his evolutionary account). I agree with much of what Dewey says. I find his separation of the religious from the supernatural compelling (because of my own individual tastes and biases). I am more than convinced that the religious quality of experience, that is, the fundamental reordering of the will as evidenced in our adjustment to some particular experience and rooted in the creative workings of the imagination, can be had apart from religion(s) of any sort.

I remember shouting a loud "yes!" when I first read these words: "They [theists and their kin] will have to ask, as far as they nominally believe in the need for radical social change, whether what they accomplish when they point with one hand to the seriousness of present evils is not undone when the other hand points away from man and nature for their remedy."[7] Perhaps this was an adolescent rebellion against my indebtedness to Cornel West, whose Kierkegaard-inspired and blues-soaked Christianity I could not embrace. Or maybe it was Dewey's unflinching faith in our capacity and responsibility to take hold of the world we inhabit. Either way I was inspired.

With Dewey our salvation or damnation remains always in our hands; it is our responsibility, our cross to bear, and we take it up with the idea that we are a part of a communion of fellows with passionate commitments that reaches back to a distant past and extends forward to generations to come. As he writes, "Ours is the responsibility of conserving, transmitting, rectifying and expanding the heritage of values we have received that those who come after us may receive it more solid and secure, more widely accessible and more generally shared than we have received it."[8] His, and by extension mine, is a practical faith in ideal ends, a faith that lights up our imagination and convicts us to act in pursuit of those ends. It is a common faith, precisely because each of us has it.

This view led me to take seriously appeals to an ethic of racial authenticity during the interwar period. Here scholars, activists, and laypersons exhibited ways of being in the world that insisted on a kind of radical responsibility rooted in a natural piety—one might even call it a blues-soaked piety—because it took shape against the background of a society committed ostensibly to democracy and to the value gap. And herein lies my unease.

My ambivalence with A Common Faith rests in my sense, a deeply felt and personal sense, I must add, that religious impulses often reside in the need for consolation: that sense of helplessness in the face of uncertainty and loss (especially in the light of violence) and the broken fragments left in its wake.[9] Here passionate, critical intelligence only takes us so far.[10] Even if we employ Dewey's inversion strategy and shift the focus of our attention to those dispositions that reflect a deep and enduring change in attitude toward the world and others, we must do so in the context of the ongoing reality of brokenness and its implications for the life lived and for a life imagined otherwise.

Obviously, William James and the particular tradition out of which I come hover in the background. James is compelling not so much because I find his talk of religious experience convincing. I don't. I do not hold the view that religious experience singles out anything unique in experience.[11] But the place from which James takes up the question—this sense that all cannot end in shipwreck, this idea that, for some, the "real core of the religious problem is a cry for Help! Help!," speaks to me profoundly.[12] It does so because of my own intimate relationship with loss and because of the fact—and it is a disconcerting fact indeed—that the people to whom I belong, not just my immediate family but those who were snatched from the shores of distant lands, have had to grapple with loss as a background condition for their efforts at self-creation and as a fundamental feature of their sojourn in this nation.

I have struggled with this issue throughout my work. My aim, for example, in In a Shade of Blue was to bring American pragmatism across the proverbial tracks to see what happens when we leave behind the narrow concerns of professional philosophy and tackle the strange experience of black folk in this country. I have experimented with this move by reading Toni Morrison's novel *Beloved* as an illustration of a pragmatic sense of the tragic. And I am currently writing about James Baldwin, a thinker who transfigures Ralph Waldo Emerson and John Dewey precisely because he wrestles with race, as an exemplar of what I call black democratic perfectionism. When it comes to the issue of African American religion and pragmatism, W. E. B. Du Bois has been at the heart of my reflections. In fact, he has hovered backstage in the previous two chapters. It is time my engagement with him come into full view.

||||||||||||||||||

I think of Du Bois as a figure that represents a third way between Dewey and James, someone who enables us to take up the religious ideal as Dewey commended and who keeps track of the need for consolation without appealing to religious metaphysical foundations that provide comfort as James insisted. We typically think about Du Bois's view of religion in light of his essay "Of the Faith of the Fathers" in his classic 1903 book *The Souls of Black Folk* or his work *The Negro Church*, published the same year. These works stand as two of the first treatments of African American religion as an object of inquiry. In "Of the Faith of the Fathers," for example, Du Bois does not take himself to be explicating the faith claims of a particular religious tradition, nor does he understand his task to involve a historical description of a particular religious denomination. Du Bois is neither a theologian nor a church historian. Instead, he sets out to examine the social history of "the Black Church" and its role in African American political life at that time.[13] This social history, of course, is written against the background of enormous challenges confronting African Americans at the dawn of the twentieth century.

Du Bois put forward a description of a dynamic social institution confronted with the enormous transformations wrought by increasing urbanization and modernization as well as the emergence of Jim Crow in the South. Changes in labor discipline and the rapid consolidation of a distinctive form of imperial whiteness (the coloniality of power) fundamentally affected the life chances of black people in this country and around the world. Du Bois asked how might this important institution (the black church), one that predated the black family, respond to the shifting material conditions of black life. Here he locates the idea of double consciousness introduced in the first chapter of *Souls* in the religious life of African Americans, folks caught in a double aim: the simultaneous rejection of American life and the desire to be included in it.[14]

In this sense, Du Bois's essay provides the narrative frame for early histories of African American religion. In addition to his account of the origins of African American religiosity and its form of expression through the preacher, the frenzy, and the music, Du Bois characterizes African American religion in terms of a conflict between those persons with religious commitments who seek refuge from the world and those who engage with it. This conflict becomes all the more acute in light of the significant transformations in black life wrought by modernization and urbanization. For him, the question confronting those religious persons was this: how might their convictions inform the kinds of political choices required by the moment of *sturm* and *drang*? On Du Bois's view, a religious orientation that was otherworldly or one focused primarily on personal gain failed to respond appropriately to the conditions of black living at the turn of the century.[15]

So much can be said here, but I am less interested in this institutional dimension of African American religion (although I understand fully the need to keep track of how religious institutions, especially in the case of African Americans, shape our lifeworld) than I am in the way Du Bois commends a particular religious disposition in response to the modernization of black life. It may be the case that we have given too much attention to his sociological treatment of the black church and its role in policing morality within black communities and not enough attention to the religious ideal he commends at the end of "Of the Faith of the Fathers."

Du Bois ends "Of the Faith of the Fathers" with a reference to a new religious ideal. He writes:

> But back of this still broods silently the deep religious feeling of the real negro heart, the stirring, unguided might of powerful human souls who have lost the guiding star of the past and are seeking in the great night *a new religious ideal*. Some day the Awakening will come, when the pent-up vigor of ten million souls shall sweep irresistibly toward the Goal, out of the Valley

of the Shadow of Death, where all *that makes life worth living*—Liberty, Justice, and Right—is marked "For White People Only."[16] [emphasis added]

The appeal to a new religious ideal is admittedly a vague gesture that lends itself to misreading. I have on occasion read it as a reinscription of a kind of essentialist idea of the inherent religiosity of black folk. The "deep religious feeling of the real negro heart," something echoed by Alain Locke two decades later, is just another instance of bad anthropology in *Souls*. But I now believe Du Bois is doing something quite different. Freed from the historical encumbrances of the past, he suggests, African Americans are now released to imagine anew and to do so in such a way that gives depth and significance to the question that William James grappled with in his classic 1895 essay "Is Life Worth Living?"[17]

For Du Bois, this question is not taken up in the abstract. He struggles with it in the context of a world darkened by the realities of white supremacy and the broken selves left in its wake. What follows "Of the Faith of the Fathers" is the essay "Of the Passing of the First-Born." The contours of the new religious ideal are given shape not in the context of grappling with religious disease but with confronting his baby in the coffin. Death, loss, and unimaginable grief constitute the background of its articulation. The idea, then, of Du Bois's religious naturalism as a kind of third way grows out of his insistence on beginning here, with brokenness and its consequences, to articulate a practical faith in ideal ends.

The last paragraph of "Of the Faith of the Fathers" sets the stage for his reflections on the death of his son—a formal elegy that offers little to no consolation to him or the reader. And it is here that I want to linger a bit, to reflect on what might it mean to foreground this essay as his account of a religious attitude instead of "Of the Faith of the Fathers." What I hope to show, and again this is all preliminary, is that Du Bois provides us with a view that can be called a "chastened pragmatic religious naturalism" and that the shift in focus from "Of the Faith" to "Of the Passing of the First-Born" may help us chart a particular mode of religious expression that goes from Du Bois to Ralph Ellison and James Baldwin all the way to Ayana Mathis and her extraordinary novel *The Twelve Tribes of Hattie*.[18]

This chastened view begins with the disturbing realization that the natural world, as it is, is in fact arrayed against one's aims and pur-poses—that the very ground upon which one stands, that into which we are thrown, is in fact diseased, distorted, and deformed, not naturally but by human actions directed toward black people.[19] Like James Baldwin, the view fully presumes that human capacities take shape in lifeworlds that often dash dreams and deny individuals dignity and standing. These are contexts that socialize individuals into doubting themselves and their abilities as well as circumstances that force people to live with the imma-nence of precarity. Baldwin's words about his brother in *The Fire Next Time* come to mind: "And, I know, which is much worse, and this is the crime of which I accuse my country and my countrymen, and for which neither I nor time nor history will ever forgive them, that they have destroyed and are destroying hundreds of thousands of lives and do not know it and do not want to know it."[20] And still that world is our foundation, the place from which we dare to forge unique selves in communion with others who are similarly situated.

This work and effort involve religious stories—narratives that orient us not only to particular problems, but to the very task of self-creation. As Jonathon Kahn notes, "Du Bois deploys religious vocabularies in order to craft a moral and political sensibility attuned to the finite needs of selves and communities struggling against concrete social and political reali-ties."[21] He does so without appeal to metaphysical foundations; instead, Du Bois keeps us squarely in what he calls in "Of Our Spiritual Strivings" the "strange experience"—that which establishes us, black folk, as the problematic in the United States.[22] He does so not to have us wallow in pessimism or self-pity or to slip into a form of sycophancy or hatred.[23] In-stead, Du Bois commends his view in light of his own distinctive melior-ist vision: that the world we inhabit can be saved, that the hell black folks catch can be undone, if we only act (without guarantee of satisfactory out-comes). Here the subjunctive mood, "that maybes are the essence of the situation," stands as a distinctive feature of an *uncommon faith*: that the "as yet" is voiced in the face of loss and horror made explicit and that "as yet" evidences itself in dispositions that disturb the world as it is (a world of actions, practices, and systems that all too often push certain alternative visions beyond the bounds of the thinkable).

What emerges in "Of the Passing of the First-Born" is a black religious attitude that aspires not for wholeness but for something "more," and it stems from the irrepressible and irrevocable fact of brokenness. It is an uncommon faith in broken, wounded selves. As Du Bois writes in *Souls*, "The bowed and bent old man cries, with thrice-repeated wail: 'O Lord, keep me from sinking down,' and he rebukes the devil of doubt who can whisper: 'Jesus is dead and God's gone away.' Yet the soul hunger is there, the restlessness of the savage, the wail of the wanderer, and the plaint is put in one little phrase, '*My soul wants something that's new, that's new.*'"[24]

Kahn makes his case for Du Bois's pragmatic religious naturalism without much attention given to "Of the Passing of the First-Born." For him, the essay is "an angry, politically engaged jeremiad on race relations."[25] Much more is going on here than this. Three moments in the essay stand out. Each illustrates a particular feature of Du Bois's uncommon faith: First, Du Bois's account rests on his meliorism, his belief that the status of the world is uncertain; it can be saved or it can go to hell depending on our choices, actions, and efforts. Second, his account embraces ambiguity and uncertainty. Du Bois insists, like James and Dewey, that the open-ended character of experience does not offer clear pathways to achieve desired ends. This makes the struggle for black freedom all the more perilous and demands a different kind of grounding for the strenuous mood. And third, in the face of his son's death, Du Bois invokes a natural piety rooted in his commitment to generations to come, a commitment pursued against the headwinds of loneliness and despair.

1. MELIORISM

Du Bois writes, "Within the Veil was he born, said I; and there within shall he live,—a Negro and a Negro's son. Holding in that little head—ah, bitterly!—the unbowed pride of a hunted race, clinging with that tiny dimpled hand—ah, wearily!—to *a hope not hopeless but unhopeful*, and seeing with those bright wondering eyes that peer into my soul a land whose freedom is to us a mockery and whose liberty a lie."[26] Here he echoes the line at the end of "Of the Faith of the Fathers," "where all that makes life worth living—Liberty, Justice, and Right—is marked 'For White People' only."

The context for his son's birth and death is a land shot through with the evil of racism, with practices that cut short the life possibilities of those on the wrong side of the veil and distort and deform the characters of those committed to such evil. But from the beginning, Du Bois provides the reader with a kind of meliorist position. Hope still resides here even in bleak times, even where death seems to be a constant companion. And like Ralph Waldo Emerson before him, Du Bois insists that when we act or experience the world in such a way that it becomes definitive of who we take ourselves to be, we do so, as Stanley Cavell writes, "in hope and on such claim to authority as only we alone, in our uncertainty, can bring to it."[27] This is practical wisdom colored a deep shade of blue. The new religious ideal is rooted in a world of action that all too often frustrates our aims and ends. We nevertheless muster the courage to act, with little to no guarantee that those actions will secure our desired aims and ends. We do so because, in the end, it is all up to us.

But we recognize that we do so as broken and fragile selves. The harshness of the world—the fact, as Toni Morrison writes in Beloved, that this world can dirty you on the inside so bad that you don't like yourself anymore—overdetermines the conditions within which we act, the very conditions that shape our striving for better selves. As a form of meliorism, we understand that the actions are those of broken, wounded souls. This fact gives the pursuit of a higher self a particular inflection. Seeking a higher self in a world that denies one standing is bad enough. But to seek that self amid the wounds and shards of a personal life lived gives new meaning to Du Bois's cry of "two unreconciled striving" that threaten to unhinge.[28]

Du Bois's position is not a view of Promethean powers deployed in a romantic act of self-creation. For him, the very reach for a higher self entails a struggle, not simply with the dangers of conformity, but with the material and psychic conditions that block the way to our understanding of who we can be and what we are capable of. The primacy of human will and practice remains, but both are shadowed by the persistence of concrete evils that often frustrate self-realization. The task is to develop one's unique talents within community and to understand those talents as gifts capable of transforming the circumstances of one's living. This is a critical point for the new religious ideal, and it bridges Dewey's faith in us and James's cry for help.

2. AMBIGUITY AND UNCERTAINTY

Du Bois writes, "She who in simple clearness of vision sees beyond the stars said when he had flown, 'He will be happy There; he ever loved beautiful things.' And I, far more ignorant, and blind by the web of mine own weaving, sit alone winding words and muttering, '*If still he be, and he be There, and there be a There, let him be happy, O Fate.*'"[29] In this pained passage, we clearly see Du Bois standing in loss, unimaginable grief, and profound uncertainty. What Arnold Rampersad described as a bitter parody of a Christian elegy is seen in the last tortured sentence. Like Emerson, Du Bois can find no consolation. In fact, he denies himself access to the comfort that the primal scene of black Christendom offers and finds himself engaged in circling spirals of grief. God offers no respite from suffering. Throughout *Souls*, the conditional "if" qualifies his invocation of God. He doesn't outright deny God's existence; he simply fails to assert God's presence in the way that is so familiar to African American religious thought. At the end of the chapter on the sorrow songs, for example, Du Bois makes explicit the conditional nature of the new ideal: "If somewhere in this whirl and chaos of things there dwells Eternal Good, pitiful yet masterful, then anon in His good time America shall rend the Veil and the prisoner shall go free."[30] So the question becomes, what does Du Bois have available to him to muster the strength to keep on living and to hold off debilitating despair?

3. NATURAL PIETY

The answer is found in his view of natural piety. Du Bois writes, "For what, forsooth, shall a negro want with pride amid the humiliations of fifty million fellows? Well sped, my boy, before the world had dubbed your ambition insolence, had held your ideals unattainable, and to you to cringe and bow. Better far this nameless void that stops my life than a sea of sorrow for you." The next sentence takes it all back: "*Idle words.*"[31] So Du Bois rejects the escapist narrative; metaphysical comfort is not his to have. Instead, he desperately reaches for what is possible, and he ascends to the subjunctive mood. Echoing Emerson's "patience, patience, up again old heart," Du Bois grasps for the possibility that all is not settled. As he writes: "Not for me,—I shall die in my bonds,—but for fresh young souls who have not known the night and waken to the morning; a morning when men ask of the workman, not 'Is he white?' but 'Can he work?' When men ask artists, not 'Are they black?' but 'Do they know?'"[32] But this move is not an easy one; it requires confronting directly the disconcerting and irrevocable fact that his son is dead.[33]

In *The Future of the Race*, Cornel West claims that this moment reveals the shortsighted vision of Du Bois: that he refused "to linger with the sheer tragedy of his son's death—without casting his son as an emblem of the race or a symbol of a black deliverance to come." For West, Du Bois doesn't grapple with "Dostoyevsky's challenge to wrestle in a sustained way with the irrevocable fact of an innocent child's death."[34] His rationalism simply gets in the way. I think the instincts of my good friend have led him to the right place, but he draws the wrong conclusion. I don't have the space to vindicate the claim here, but I would suggest that Du Bois's embrace of the subjunctive mood in this moment—his voicing of possibility—reveals the depth of his chastened pragmatic religious naturalism. Du Bois doesn't have the security of West's Christianity.

In this darkest of moments, when confronted with the fact that his son is dead, unlike William James, Du Bois does not ponder suicide (so far as we know). Instead, he finds consolation, like Thomas Carlyle before him, in transforming grief into struggle.[35] He finds the courage to stake his life on the possibility that one day the reality of racism will no longer be and those young souls might be able to simply be! William James argued that such an act was one of religious faith—the belief that possibility exists is religious faith.[36] This is especially so when darkness surrounds one (when it seems that "hope unborn has died").

But this is not all: Du Bois doesn't leave his son behind. He still grieves at the end of the essay. "Of the Passing of the First-Born," is followed by essays of death ("Of Alexander Crummell" and "Of the Coming of John," in which Du Bois recasts Emerson's secret melancholy and Thoreau's quiet desperation in the full light of the brutal realities of race in this country). In the end Du Bois's chastened pragmatic religious naturalism keeps in view the desperate cry for help that so motivated William James.

But he does so in light of actual problems and practices that cut short the lives of those who live behind the veil or who are simply out of sight and willfully ignored.

This is the power of his religious naturalism: that he gives voice to the "as yet" while struggling with the devastation of loss. To my mind, it is an uncommon faith in the capacities of broken people, those who have been profoundly wounded by the reality of white supremacy in this country, to seek better and more excellent versions of who they take themselves to be. And in the very act of doing so, of seeking an individuality amid the traps of an ideology that sets who we are in stone, those broken people dare to upend everything. Or as James Baldwin put it, "When a black man, whose destiny and identity have always been controlled by others, decides and states that he will control his own destiny and rejects the identity given to him by others, he is talking revolution."[37]

llllllllllllllllllll

I believe this uncommon faith has had an enduring presence in African American life. One can trace it from Du Bois to James Baldwin, Toni Morrison, and Ayana Mathis.[38] Mathis's first novel, *The Twelve Tribes of Hattie*, stands as a particularly powerful example of this view. The novel opens with Hattie nursing her twins who are dying of pneumonia in the bathroom of an unheated home in Philadelphia. The setting announces up front that it seeks to question the moral of the migration story: the North wasn't an uncomplicated place of freedom. Illusions shatter all around her. With the death of her babies, something breaks inside Hattie, and the shards wound, especially her subsequent children.

Each chapter charts the aftermath, the ongoing devastation that followed from that initial irrevocable moment of loss and grief. At the end of the novel it seems, finally, the generational evil that has so consumed Hattie will not touch her granddaughter, Sala. God's grace, we are led to believe, will protect her. But as Sala prepared to join the church, Hattie said, "No."

> The sanctuary was silent. Hattie pulled her granddaughter down the center aisle. She couldn't allow it. She had lost Six to the altar. She sent him off to Alabama with nothing but a Bible, and he had become a womanizer and an imposter. By the time she understood the depth of his unhappiness, it had

been too late to save him. Her twins were dead. She had given Ella back to Georgia. It was too late for Cassie, whom Hattie had also sent away. And it was too late for Hattie, who was a fraud in Christ and had shown Sala the ways of fraudulence. She couldn't bear that the child was already so broken she was driven to the mercy seat. There was time for Sala. Hattie didn't know how to save her granddaughter. . . . Here we are sixty years out of Georgia, she thought, a new generation has been born and there's still the same wounding and the same pain. I can't allow it. . . . Hattie looked around at the disapproving faces of the congregation. Their indignation would pass—everything passed sooner or later—and if it didn't, she would give up the church too, this dear comfort of her old age. She was not too old to weather another sacrifice. Hattie put her arm around Sala and pulled her close; she patted her granddaughter's back roughly, unaccustomed as she was to tenderness.[39]

Here Mathis rewrites the primal scene of African American life: Mama's slap of Beneatha in Lorraine Hansberry's *A Raisin in the Sun*, James Baldwin's John on the thrashing floor in *Go Tell It on the Mountain*. Mathis cuts off the retreat to a kind of religious metaphysical comfort, and instead we are left with fragile, finite, and in some cases, broken selves working for our children and our children's children to secure the values that we have come to cherish. With a hope not hopeless but unhopeful found in that awkward moment of tenderness, care, and grief, Hattie gives powerful expression to an uncommon faith.

||||||||||||||||

Perhaps I can make this point clearer by turning to the internationally acclaimed Ghanaian artist El Anatsui and his Broken Pots series. (These are the images that separate each of the preceding chapters.) He takes the fragments and shards of broken clay pots and gives them depth and form. The result is something profoundly beautiful. The broken pot, in his hands, does not represent a permanent state of brokenness; rather, its transformation from that relegated to the trash bin to that which is beautiful metaphorically reflects our individual ability to pick up the pieces and to reach for a higher self—a *reconstructed perfectionism*. As Olu Oguibe puts it, "Leak as we may, we nevertheless continue to mend."[40] Here wholeness is not the objective.[41] Our original form is forever in abeyance. Instead, at the moment of the transformational wound, a different way of being in the world is made possible, and it is within this space of brokenness we make ourselves and the world anew.

This is the uncommon faith that Du Bois called his new religious ideal: a kind of black perfectionism that begins with brokenness. Here one refuses to view wound and brokenness as a permanent fixed state and aspires instead to something "more"—where a relentless faith in the possible, without metaphysical guarantees, evidences itself in radical dispositions toward the world as it is, toward those who would do anything to keep it that way, and in the service of the world as it could be. This uncommon faith requires a different kind of self-love and self-trust. Baby Suggs's sermon in Morrison's *Beloved* powerfully expresses the point:

> Here . . . in this place, we flesh; flesh that weeps, laughs; flesh that dances on bare feet in grass. Love it. Love it hard. Yonder they do not love your flesh. They despise it. They don't love your eyes; they'd just as soon pick em out. No more do they love the skin on your back. Yonder they flay it. And O my people they do not love your hands. Those they only use, tie, bind, chop off and leave empty. Love your hands! Love them. Raise them up and kiss them. Touch others with them, pat them together, stroke them on your face 'cause they don't love that either. You got to love it, you! And no, they ain't in love with your mouth. Yonder, out there, they will see it broken and break it again. What you say out of it they will not heed. What you scream from it they do not hear. What you put into it to nourish your body they will snatch away and give you leavins instead. No, they don't love your mouth. You got to love it. This is flesh I'm talking about here. Flesh that needs to be loved. Feet that need to rest and to dance; backs that need support; shoulders that need arms, strong arms I'm telling you. And O my people, out yonder, hear me, they do not love your neck unnoosed and straight. So love your neck; put a hand on it, grace it, stroke it and hold it up. And all your inside parts that they'd just as soon slop for hogs, you got to love them. The dark, dark lover—love it, love it and the beat and beating heart, love that too. More than lungs that have yet to draw free air. More than your life-holding womb and your life-giving private parts, hear me now, love your heart. For this is the prize.[42]

This is what Hattie hoped to bequeath to Sala. It is the love Du Bois, as he grieved for his baby, commended to us: that out of the broken fragments of the life lived those very shards would provide a foundation, without the security of comforting illusions, to step forward and dare to be, wounds and all. That is revolution. That is an uncommon faith.

El Anatsui, *Chambers of Memory*, 1977, ceramic and manganese,
16 × 11 × 10½ inches. © El Anatusi, Courtesy of the artist and
Jack Shainman Gallery, New York.

NOTES

INTRODUCTION
PRAGMATIC BEGINNINGS

1. West, *American Evasion of Philosophy*, 5.
2. Dewey, *Influence of Darwin on Philosophy*, 17.

CHAPTER 1
PRAGMATISM AND
AFRICAN AMERICAN RELIGION

1. James, *Pragmatism*, 28.
2. Dewey, "Context and Thought," 19.
3. Rorty, *Consequences of Pragmatism*, xlii.
4. This is not to deny the importance of those churches in black social and political life.
5. Dewey, *Common Faith*, 14.
6. Ibid., 17. Emphasis mine.
7. Ibid., 14.
8. Raboteau, *Slave Religion*, 306.
9. Dewey, *Common Faith*, 16.
10. Du Bois, *Souls of Black Folk*, 364.
11. Ibid., 395.
12. Dewey, *Common Faith*, 17.
13. Fesmire, *John Dewey and Moral Imagination*, 65.
14. James, *Will to Believe*, 90.
15. Acts 2:12–13.

CHAPTER 2
BABEL IN THE NORTH

1. White, *Content of the Form*, 60–61.
2. Orsi, *Between Heaven and Earth*, 178.
3. Scott, "History-Writing as Critique."
4. Oakeshott, *On History and Other Essays*, xii.
5. Oakeshott, *Experience and Its Modes*, 85.
6. Mead, "Nature of the Past," 346.
7. Adorno, *Critical Models*, 155.
8. Wilmore, *Black Religion and Black Radicalism*, 162.
9. Ibid., 164.
10. Sernett, *Bound for the Promised Land*, 184.
11. Burkett, "Baptist Church," 135.
12. Sernett, *Bound for the Promised Land*, 184–87.
13. Wilmore, *Black Religion and Black Radicalism*, 162.
14. "Miles Mark Fisher, himself a Baptist preacher, characterized the state of African American religion prior to the Great Migration era: 'Prior to the world-war the negro preacher was expounding otherworldly topics in addition to an occasional sensational or practical sermon.'" Quoted in Sernett, *Bound for the Promised Land*, 121.
15. Lincoln and Mamiya, *Black Church*, 121.
16. Stout, *Ethics after Babel*, 72.
17. Ibid., 79.
18. Casanova, *Public Religion*, 13.
19. C. Eric Lincoln and Lawrence Mamiya in *The Black Church in the African American Experience* describe this process as a result of partial differentiation. For them, "partial differentiation emphasizes the continuous interaction and interrelationships between churches and areas like politics, economics, education, and culture. The view of the complete differentiation of religion, a withdrawal into a private religious sphere which is prevalent in the social sciences, leads to a misunderstanding of the role of black churches in urban society" (123). On their view, the established black churches were affected by the differentiation, stratification, and pluralism that the urban environment encouraged, but this fact should not lead us to overemphasize the competition of these various sectors with the church or to embrace a hard distinction between the sacred and the secular. My use of "secularization" rejects traditional understandings of the term. I am not claiming that religion is regulated to some private domain. Instead, secularization takes place in the way people deliberate about public matters (the sorts of languages that emerge to bridge stratification, plurality, and differentiation). As for Mamiya and Lincoln's use of the phrase "partial differentiation," I am content to think about it pragmatically: what difference would it practically make to use the phrase

"partial differentiation" as opposed to "secularization" per my understanding of the term? If no practical difference can be found, then the two alternatives mean practically the same the thing.

20. Harrison, *When Africa Awakes*, 76.

21. It is important that we do not understand this language as somehow obliterating all differences in the black communities. Class, gender, and cultural differences remained and often exerted tremendous pressures on the conversation. As Peter Gottlieb notes, "tensions that arose from growing differences of class within the African-American population were not overcome by the rising awareness of a common racial identity, actively promoted by the Pittsburgh Courier and by some prominent figures in the community." The point I am making, however, is that the language of the conversation within which those tensions were expressed was often that of racial authenticity. See Gottlieb's "Rethinking the Great Migration," 74.

Such a view could help us understand, for example, Martin Luther King Jr.'s failure in the North as, in part, a discursive one. He continued to ground his public utterances in his religious belief. Or we can think of the failure of Malcolm X's initial religious effort, the Muslim Mosque Incorporated, and the subsequent "secular" Organization of African American Unity as examples of the discursive requirements of the black North.

22. Burkett, *Garveyism as a Religious Movement*, 56.

23. Locke, "New Negro," 53.

24. Ibid., 53. Emphasis mine.

25. Ibid., 50.

26. Hughes, "Negro Artist," 306.

27. Burkett, *Garveyism as a Religious Movement*, 56.

28. Kelley, *Race Rebels*, 120.

29. Ibid., 115.

30. Imani Perry's brilliant book *May We Forever Stand* offers a stunning account of the role of these reconfigured institutions in black life as she charts the history of "Lift Every Voice and Sing."

31. Higginbotham, "Rethinking Vernacular Culture," 159.

32. Not only must we disentangle theories of secularization from claims about the would-be erosion and decline of religion but we must also inquire into the effects of processes of modern differentiation and all they entail on the way we talk about moral matters. In other words, once we get rid of "the confusion of historical processes of secularization proper with the alleged and anticipated consequences which those processes [are] supposed to have upon religion" (see Casanova, *Public Religion*, 19), then we can get about the business of attending to the transformations of moral languages and moral communities. That is, we can get about the business of "reflexive ethnography."

33. Higginbotham, "Rethinking Vernacular Culture," 171. Just as Benjamin

Elijah Mays singles out the unchurched, secular black person as a distinctive character in The Negro's God, I want to suggest that the religious person is also a distinct character of this period. Without differentiation unleashed by modernization, there is no need to set oneself apart in this way.

CHAPTER 3

AN UNCOMMON FAITH

1. Dewey, "Context and Thought," 19.

2. Ibid., 11.

3. Ibid., 11.

4. Ibid., 12.

5. Ibid., 14.

6. Ibid., 16.

7. Dewey, Common Faith, 82.

8. Ibid., 87.

9. I invoke "wake" in the sense that Christina Sharpe uses it in her book In the Wake. For her, the word works on three registers: (1) as the path behind a ship, (2) as a form of keeping watch over the dead, and (3) as a mode of coming to consciousness. And the idea of brokenness is indebted to the work of Hortense Spillers and her account of "wounding" in "Mama's Baby, Papa's Maybe."

10. Dewey's relative silence about the death of his sons, Morris (died of diphtheria in 1895) and Gordon (typhoid fever in 1905), in some ways reveals the limit of appeals to critical intelligence in such situations. We find nothing in Dewey's corpus akin to Emerson's grappling with the death of Waldo or W. E. B. Du Bois's struggle with the death of Burghardt. I need to think more carefully about his silence; it may reveal that Dewey himself understood the limits of critical intelligence when faced with such tragic moments.

11. Dewey writes, "the actual religious quality in the experienced described is the effect produced, the better adjustment in life and its conditions, not the manner and cause of its production. The way in which the experience operated, its function, determines its religious value" (A Common Faith, 14).

12. James, Varieties of Religious Experience, 181.

13. William Hart offers a wonderful analysis of Du Bois's account in his important essay, "Three Rival Narratives of Black Religion."

14. "The worlds within and without the Veil of Color are changing, and changing rapidly, but not at the same rate, not in the same way; and this must produce a peculiar wrenching of the soul, a peculiar sense of doubt and bewilderment. Such a double life, with double thoughts, double duties, and double social classes, must give rise to double words and double ideals, and tempt the mind to pretence or to revolt, to hypocrisy or to radicalism." Du Bois, Souls of Black Folk, 502.

15. Du Bois wrote: "Between the two extreme types of ethical attitude which I have thus sought to make clear waves the mass of millions of Negroes, North and South; and their religious life and activity partake of this social conflict within their ranks. Their churches are differentiating,—now into groups of cold fashionable devotees, in no way distinguishable from similar white groups in color of skin; now into large social and business institutions catering to the desire for information and amusement of their members, warily avoiding unpleasant questions both within and without the black world, and preaching in effect if not in word: Dum vivimus, vivamus." Du Bois, Souls of Black Folk, 504–5.

16. Du Bois, Souls of Black Folk, 505.

17. First delivered at the YMCA of Harvard University and the Philadelphia Society of Ethical Culture. Later published in the International Journal of Ethics in 1895.

18. Jonathon Kahn notes, "Pragmatic religious naturalists subvert traditional religious metaphysics of ultimate truth and foundational beliefs while holding tight to religious stories, moods, symbols, rhetoric, and moral values because they are links to the past, because they are powerful tools and narratives for shaping and envisioning life, and because they can allow for a type of spirituality that emphasizes fallibility, fragility, and the power of the human made ties that bind us and make us dependent on each other." Kahn, Divine Discontent, 13.

Much has been written on Du Bois and pragmatism (pro and con). Recent work has taken up the question of Du Bois and religion. Past characterizations of him have ranged from that he is an atheist to he is an agnostic; most commentators find his religious references a bit puzzling. But I think Herbert Aptheker was right: "The impression exists that Dr. Du Bois was areligious or even antireligious. The facts are otherwise." Edward Blum's W. E. B. Du Bois, American Prophet does a great job of showing how Christianity animates Du Bois's work. But I must say that the best work on Du Bois and religion is the excellent book by Jonathon Kahn, Divine Discontent. He follows the path of the late Manning Marable's wonderful essay "The Black Faith of W. E. B. Du Bois."

19. Du Bois's pragmatism has several dimensions: (1) the problematic located in what he calls "strange experience"; (2) an insistence on historical consciousness (where double consciousness is both a historical product and the site for the exercise of critical intelligence); (3) a presupposed protean self (he follows Emerson here but with a significant difference: his self is fraught with the challenges of the environment within which that self takes shape—fluid/ambiguous/conflicted); (4) the connection between material conditions and our idea of the good; and (5) a commitment to democracy alongside a deep suspicion of liberalism.

20. Baldwin, Fire Next Time, 5.

21. Kahn, Divine Discontent, 11.

22. I like to think of this alongside Heidegger's Unheimlichkeit.

23. One might include Ta-Nehisi Coates's recent work here. He is adamant in his atheism, and what seems to follow from that, he believes, is the illusion of hope. In effect, he resigns himself to the reality of white supremacy. But giving up on metaphysical foundations does not necessarily lead us down such a path. In fact, Du Bois demonstrates otherwise.

24. Du Bois, *Souls of Black Folk*, 542.

25. Kahn, *Divine Discontent*, 50. This may be a bit too strong. Kahn does find valuable the formulation "hope not hopeless but unhopeful" (44).

26. Du Bois, *Souls of Black Folk*, 507.

27. Cavell, "Hope Against Hope," in *Emerson's Transcendental Etudes*, 182. Shannon Mariotti writes, "For Cavell, Emerson constantly circles toward this greater intimacy with reality: we cannot move closer to the universal by clutching and grasping, but only by abandoning the self to what is next." She goes on to describe Emerson's perfectionism "as a continual process of transformation of both the self and the world, whereby we, in circling spirals that never end, continually project the world we think, the world we imagine and dream of, as the possibility for the world we now live, as the possible next." Mariotti suggests that this circling "gets in the way of [Emerson's] ability to grieve." Perhaps. But I want to suggest that Du Bois is doing something similar here and grief is its spur. See Mariotti, "On the Passing," 359.

28. See Cavell's *Conditions Handsome and Unhandsome*. For Emerson, each of us has the task before us to ascend to higher forms of excellence. But this task isn't rooted in some fixed destination or some final resting place of perfection. That final resting place differs for each person. Life's journey consists of better and more excellent versions of who we take ourselves to be. Each calls us to a higher sense of ourselves and requires the abandonment of older versions. My colleague and good friend Jeffrey Stout puts it best: "the higher self congeals out of the highest intimations of excellence you can intuit from where you stand. Excellence and sacred value are the kinds of goodness that matter most for living well." See Stout and Kuipers, "Excellence and the Emersonian Perfectionist."

29. Du Bois, *Souls of Black Folk*, 509. Emphasis mine.

30. Ibid., 545.

31. Ibid., 510. Emphasis mine.

32. Ibid., 510.

33. Reminded of Howard Thurman's talk of accepting our fact. There is the relationship to death in African American letters that throws us back into the messiness of life. James Baldwin's powerful formulation in *The Fire Next Time* comes to mind: "Perhaps the whole root of our trouble, the human trouble, is that we will sacrifice all the beauty of our lives, will imprison ourselves in totems, taboos, crosses, blood sacrifices, steeples, mosques, races, armies, flags, nations, in order to deny the fact of death, the only fact we have. It seems to me that one ought

to rejoice in the fact of death—ought to decide, indeed, to earn one's death by confronting with passion the conundrum of life" (91–92). But it is in the actual facing of the fact that life is given depth and meaning. Evasions leave us in a hall of mirrors with illusions guiding our path forward or backward or nowhere at all.

34. West and Gates, *Future of the Race*, 63.

35. West only sees Carlyle's imprint in Du Bois's insistence on the talented tenth. But the impress of Carlyle can be seen here: that Du Bois would transform melancholic pessimism into protest.

36. Levinson, *Religious Investigations of William James*, 31.

37. Baldwin, "Black Power," 81.

38. A moment in James Baldwin's *Tell Me How Long the Train's Been Gone*: "A faint breeze struck, but did not cool my Ethiopian brow. Ethiopia's hands: to what god indeed, out of this despairing place, was I to stretch these hands? But I also felt, incorrigible, hoping to be reconciled, and yet unable to accept the terms of any conceivable reconciliation, that any god daring to presume that I would stretch out my hands to him would be struck by these hands with all my puny, despairing power; would be forced to confront, in these, my hands, the monstrous blood-guiltiness of God. No. I had had quite enough of God—more than enough, more than enough, the horror filled my nostrils, I gagged on the blood-drenched name; and yet was forced to see that this horror, precisely, accomplished His reality and undid my unbelief" (98).

39. Mathis, *Twelve Tribes of Hattie*, 242–43.

40. Oguibe, "El Anatsui," 52.

41. I am answering a formulation Toni Morrison offered in 1977. She talks about the aspiration to wholeness: "Each of us is in some way at some moment a victim in no position to do a thing about. Some child is always left unpicked up at some moment. In a world like that, how does one remain whole—is it just impossible to do that?" I am suggesting that the aspiration to wholeness is misguided; beauty is found elsewhere in the life we make with the pieces. See Baker-man, "Seams Can't Show: An Interview with Toni Morrison," in Taylor-Guthrie, *Conversations with Toni Morrison*, 40.

42. Morrison, *Beloved*, 88–89.

BIBLIOGRAPHY

Adorno, Theodor. *Critical Models: Interventions and Catchwords.* New York: Columbia
    University Press, 1998.
Baldwin, James. *Tell Me How Long the Train's Been Gone.* New York: Vintage, 1998.
———. *The Fire Next Time.* New York: Vintage Books, 1993.
———. "Black Power." In *The Cross of Redemption: Uncollected Writings,* edited by
    Randall Kenan, 80–85. New York: Pantheon, 2010.
Best, Wallace. *Passionately Human, No Less Divine: Religion and Culture in Black
    Chicago, 1915–1952.* Princeton: Princeton University Press, 2005.
Blum, Edward. *W. E. B. Du Bois, American Prophet.* Philadelphia: University of
    Pennsylvania Press, 2007.
Burkett, Randall. "The Baptist Church in the Years of Crisis: J. C. Austin and the
    Pilgrim Baptist Church, 1926–1950. In *African American Christianity: Essays in
    History,* edited by Paul E. Johnson, 134–58. Berkeley: University of California
    Press, 1994.
———. *Garveyism as a Religious Movement.* Metuchen, N.J.: Scarecrow Press, 1978.
Casanova, Jose. *Public Religion in the Modern World.* Chicago: University of Chicago
    Press, 1994.
Cavell, Stanley. *Conditions Handsome and Unhandsome.* Chicago: University of
    Chicago Press, 1991.
———. *Emerson's Transcendental Etudes.* Stanford, Calif.: Stanford University Press,
    2003.
Dewey, John. *A Common Faith.* New Haven, Conn.: Yale University Press, 1934.
———. "Context and Thought." In *John Dewey: The Later Works, 1925–1953,* vol.
    6: 1931–1932, edited by Jo Ann Boydston, 3–21. Carbondale: Southern Illinois
    University Press, 1989.
———. *The Influence of Darwin on Philosophy and Other Essays in Contemporary
    Thought.* New York: Henry Holt, 1910.
Du Bois, W. E. B. *Souls of Black Folk.* In *W. E. B. Du Bois: Writings,* edited by Nathan
    Huggins, 357–548. New York: Library of America, 1995.

Fauset, Arthur. *Black Gods of the Metropolis: Negro Religious Cults in the Urban North.* Philadelphia: University of Pennsylvania Press, 1944.

Fesmire, Steven. *John Dewey and Moral Imagination: Pragmatism in Ethics.* Bloomington: Indiana University Press, 2003.

Glaude, Eddie. *African American Religion: A Very Short Introduction.* New York: Oxford University Press, 2014.

———. *Exodus!: Religion, Race, and Nation in Early Nineteenth-Century Black America.* Chicago: University of Chicago Press, 2000.

———. *In a Shade of Blue: Pragmatism and the Politics of Black America.* Chicago: University of Chicago Press, 2007.

Gottlieb, Peter. "Rethinking the Great Migration: A Perspective from Pittsburgh." In *The Great Migration in Historical Perspective: New Dimensions of Race, Class, and Gender,* edited by William Joe Trotter, 68–82. Bloomington: Indiana University Press, 1991.

Harrison, Hubert. *When Africa Awakes.* New York: Porro Press, 1920.

Hart, William David. *Afro-Eccentricity: Beyond the Standard Narrative of Black Religion.* New York: Palgrave Macmillan, 2011.

———. "Three Rival Narratives of Black Religion." In *A Companion to African-American Studies,* edited by Lewis R. Gordon and Jane Anna Gordon, 476–94. Hoboken, N.J.: Blackwell, 2006.

Higginbotham, Evelyn Brooks. "Rethinking Vernacular Culture." In *The House that Race Built: Black Americans, U.S. Terrain,* edited by Wahneema Lubiano, 157–77. New York: Pantheon, 1997.

Hughes, Langston. "The Negro Artist and the Racial Mountain." In *Voices from the Harlem Renaissance,* edited by Nathan Huggins. New York: Oxford University, 1995.

James, Williams. *Pragmatism.* Indianapolis: Hackett, 1981.

———. *The Varieties of Religious Experience.* New York: Modern Library, 1999.

———. *The Will to Believe and Other Essays in Popular Philosophy.* New York: Longmans Green, 1907.

Kahn, Jonathon. *Divine Discontent: The Religious Imagination of W. E. B. Du Bois.* New York: Oxford University Press, 2009.

Kelley, Robin D. G. *Race Rebels: Culture, Politics and the Black Working Class.* New York: Free Press, 1994.

Levinson, Henry. *The Religious Investigations of William James.* Chapel Hill: University of North Carolina Press, 2011.

Lincoln, C. Eric, and Lawrence H. Mamiya. *The Black Church in the African American Experience.* Durham, N.C.: Duke University Press, 1990.

Locke, Alain. "The New Negro." In *Voices from the Harlem Renaissance,* edited by Nathan Huggins, 47–71. New York: Oxford University, 1995.

Marable, Manning. "The Black Faith of W. E. B. Du Bois: Sociocultural and

Political Dimensions of Black Religion." *Southern Quarterly* 23, no. 3 (1985): 15-55.

Mariotti, Shannon. "On the Passing of the First-Born Son: Emerson's 'Focal Distancing,' Du Bois' 'Second Sight,' and Disruptive Particularity." *Political Theory* 37, no. 3 (2009): 351–74.

Martin, Lerone. *Preaching on Wax: The Phonograph and the Making of Modern African American Religion.* New York: New York University Press, 2014

Mathis, Ayana. *The Twelve Tribes of Hattie.* New York: Vintage, 2013.

McWilliams, Susan J. *A Political Companion to James Baldwin.* Lexington: University of Kentucky Press, 2017.

Mead, George Herbert. "The Nature of the Past." In *George Herbert Mead: Selected Writings,* edited by Andrew J. Reck, 345–54. Chicago: University of Chicago Press, 1964.

Moses, Wilson. *The Golden Age of Black Nationalism, 1850–1925.* New York: Oxford University, 1978.

Morrison, Toni, ed. *Baldwin: Collected Essays.* New York: The Library of America, 1998.

———. *Beloved.* New York: Vintage, 2004.

Oakeshott, Michael. *Experience and Its Modes.* New York: Cambridge University Press, 2015.

———. *On History and Other Essays.* Indianapolis: Liberty Fund, 1999.

Oguibe, Olu. "El Anatsui: Beyond Death and Nothingness." *African Arts,* Winter 1998: 48–55.

Orsi, Robert. *Between Heaven and Earth: The Religious Worlds People Make and the Scholars Who Study Them.* Princeton, N.J.: Princeton University Press, 2005.

Raboteau, Albert. *Slave Religion: The Invisible Institution in Antebellum South.* New York: Oxford University Press, 1978.

Reck, Andrew J., ed. *George Herbert Mead: Selected Writings.* Chicago: University of Chicago Press, 1964.

Rorty, Richard. *Consequences of Pragmatism: Essays, 1972–1980.* Minneapolis: University of Minnesota Press, 1989.

Savage, Barbara. *Your Spirits Walk Beside Us: The Politics of Black Religion.* Cambridge, Mass.: Harvard University Press, 2008.

Schneedwind, J. B. "Moral Knowledge and Moral Principles." In *Revisions: Changing Perspectives in Moral Philosophy,* edited by Stanley Hauerwas and Alasdair MacIntyre, 113–26. Notre Dame, Ind.: University of Notre Dame Press, 1983.

Scott, Joan. "History-Writing as Critique." In *Manifestos for History,* edited by Keith Jenkins, Sue Morgan, and Alum Munslow, 19–38. London: Routledge, 2007.

Sernett, William. *Bound for the Promised Land: African American Religion and the Great Migration.* Durham, N.C.: Duke University Press, 1997.

Sharpe, Christina. *In the Wake: On Blackness and Being*. Durham, N.C.: Duke University Press, 2016.

Sorett, Josef. *Spirit in the Dark: A Religious History of Racial Aesthetics*. New York: Oxford University Press, 2016.

Spillers, Hortense. *Black, White, and In Color: Essays on American Culture and Literature*. Chicago: University of Chicago Press, 2003.

———. "Mama's Baby, Papa's Maybe: An American Grammar Book." Special issue, *Culture and Countermemory. Diacritics* 17, no. 2 (Summer 1987): 64–81.

Stout, Jeffrey. *Ethics after Babel: The Languages of Morals and Their Discontents*. Boston: Beacon Press, 1988.

Stout, Jeffrey, and Ron Kuipers. "Excellence and the Emersonian Perfectionist: An Interview with Jeffrey Stout, Part I." *Other Journal* 16 (2009). https:// theotherjournal.com/2009/09/01/excellence-and-the-emersonian -perfectionist-an-interview-with-jeffrey-stout-part-i/.

Taylor, Charles. *The Ethics of Authenticity*. Cambridge, Mass.: Harvard University Press, 1992.

Taylor-Guthrie, Danielle, ed. *Conversations with Toni Morrison*. Jackson: University Press of Mississippi, 1994.

Weisenfeld, Judith. *New World A-Coming: Black Religion and Racial Identity during the Great Migration*. New York: New York University Press, 2017.

West, Cornel. *The American Evasion of Philosophy: A Genealogy of Pragmatism*. Madison: University of Wisconsin Press, 1989.

West, Cornel, and Henry Louis Gates Jr. *The Future of the Race*. New York: Alfred Knopf, 1996.

White, Hayden. *The Content of the Form: Narrative Discourse and Historical Representation*. Baltimore: Johns Hopkins University Press, 1987.

———. *Tropics of Discourse: Essays in Cultural Criticism*. Baltimore: Johns Hopkins University Press, 1978.

Wilmore, Gayraud. *Black Religion and Black Radicalism: An Interpretation of the Religious History of Afro-American People*. New York: Orbis, 1984.

INDEX